Bertso Eskolak

Basque Improvisational Poetry Schools

Bidart Family Collection No.2

Bertso Eskolak Basque Improvisational Poetry Schools

Editors

Larraitz Ariznabarreta, Iñaki Arrieta Baro, Xabier Irujo

Center for Basque Studies
University of Nevada, Reno
2022

Library of Congress Cataloging-in-Publication Data

Names:
Ariznabarreta, Larraitz, editor. | Arrieta Baro, Iñaki, 1976- editor. | Irujo Ametzaga, Xabier, editor.

Title:
Bertso eskolak / Larraitz Ariznabarreta, Iñaki Arrieta Baro, Xabier Irujo.

Description: Reno : Center for Basque Studies Press, [2022] |

Series:
Conference books series | Includes bibliographical references.
| Summary: "A conference book about the schools that specialize in Basque improvised verse singing"

Provided by publisher.
Identifiers: LCCN 2022012381 | ISBN 9781949805642 (Paperback)

Subjects: LCSH: Folk poetry, Basque--History and criticism. | Poetry--Study and teaching--Spain--País Vasco. | Poetry--Study and teaching--France--Pays Basque. | Folk songs, Basque--Spain--País Vasco--History and criticism. | Folk songs, Basque--France--Pays Basque--History and criticism. | Improvisation (Music) | LCGFT: Essays.

Classification:
LCC PH5290 .B47 2022 | DDC 899/.921--dc23/eng/20220517 LC record available at https://lccn.loc.gov/2022012381

Contents

Introduction. 7

Bertsolaritza: Beyond Transmission and Preservation
Oihana Iguaran Barandiaran 15

The Possible Impact and Benefits of a Self-Organized and Structured Bertso-Eskola on the Region and on the Bertso Community
Jone Uria Albizuri 49

Beyond Linguistic Practices: Verse Schools as Prime Locus for the Co-construction of Youth Identity and Linguistics Identity
Miren Artetxe Sarasola 73

Bertsolaritza in Navarre: From the Past to the Present
Julio Soto Ezkurdia. 99

Learning about Art and the Art of Learning
Maialen Lujanbio 125

Improvisation and Life: The Oholtza Project as an Example of New Artistic Proposals for Bertsolaris
Beñat Krolem 153

A Coda
Larraitz Ariznabarreta 177

Appendix: Women Bertsolaris in a Time of Nuances: Bodies, Voices and the Art of Improvisation. An Interview with Maialen Lujanbio and Miren Artetxe
Reyes Lázaro, Jacqueline Urla 187

Introduction

In February 2018, nine hundred people gathered in Elko, Nevada, to listen to four Basque bertsolaris (Basque improvisational poets) sing in Basque. This event was part of a conference organized by the Center for Basque Studies and the Basque Library of the University of Nevada, Reno, in collaboration with the organizers of the Thirty-Fourth National Cowboy Poetry Gathering.

The 2018 Elko Basque Festival (January 29–February 4) was focused on "the contributions of Basques in the West" and included sessions on Basque arborglyphs (tree carvings), Basque poetry, Basque writing, and the experience of Basques in ranching, featuring the insight of longtime Nevada resident and stalwart of Winnemucca's Basque community, Frank Bidart—only ninety-five years young! Maialen Lujanbio, the bearer of the current bertsolaritza world champion beret, said to a reporter on the Elko Daily, "[Bertsolaritza] is a traditional but contemporary art, and I think it is one of the most powerful meeting points for Basque speakers. We hope to show our way of singing, our improvising tradition and above all our language. The Basque language [. . .] is our main tool to create our poetry, in which we express our opinions, feelings and our point of view towards any current affairs."[1]

The success of that first conference encouraged us to organize a second summit on the process of learning how to become a bertsolari. On this occasion, we focused our efforts on the bertso-eskolak, or schools for improvisational poetry. In addition to the technicalities of the process of learning how to become an improvisational poet, we also explored the bertso schools' many social, cultural, and pedagogical developments. The resulting collection emphasized the relevance of, and social impact resulting from, a large number of minors spending their

1 "Champion bertsolari to perform improvised Basque verse at gathering," *Elko Daily*, January 28, 2018. http://elkodaily.com/entertainment/champion-bertsolari-to-perform-improvised-basque-verse-at-gathering/article_9de92233-872a-51bc-b701-eb237c7705bf.html.

time—and a substantial portion of their childhood—involved with bertso poetry.

The project was made possible thanks to the sensible vision and generous contribution of the Bidart family, who are the heart of this initiative.

Just when we were awaiting the arrival of our guest presenters, on March 11, 2020, President Trump announced the travel ban for European countries. We were forced to cancel the conference on bertso-eskolak. The cancellation had been a possibility for weeks, a menace always on our minds—even as we continued to plan travel, reserve rooms, and design a website for the conference. This news, however, solidified that it was indeed impossible to guarantee the speakers from the Basque Country would be able to arrive in Reno. Nor could we assure that the University of Nevada, Reno campus would be open on April 9 and 10, when the conference was initially planned. As happened with so many events worldwide during the spring and summer of 2020, the Conference on Schools for Basque Improvisational Poetry was cancelled.

The next days were filled composing and sending messages to inform speakers, sponsors, and other stakeholders on the decision made; cancelling plane tickets, lunches, and venue reservations; and dismantling every small piece that comprises a conference. Simultaneously, the staff at the Center for Basque Studies and the Basque Library were taking the necessary steps to be prepared for a closure that finally happened on March 13.

After these unfortunate events, our goal has been to maintain the momentum achieved in the previous months and to continue supporting research and scholarly conversations on the field of bertsolaritza, even if we were unable to physically unite. We wanted to assure that we were prepared to hold the conference in the future and provide access to the research output that it enabled. Therefore, we asked the invited speakers to continue working on their presentations and papers. The volume in your hands is the fruit of that effort.

Oihana Iguaran's opening chapter provides a general framework for understanding the bertso-eskolak, the Basque improvisational poetry schools. Bertsolaritza (bertsolarism or Basque improvisational poetry) is an oral tradition passed on through generations. However, its transmission cannot be taken for granted. Bertsozale Elkartea (Association of Friends of Bertsolaritza) was created in 1985 with the primary aim of preserving this oral tradition. Hoping to counter the widespread belief that a bertsolari's talent is innate, many bertso-eskolak were set up in different towns where, in partnership with local educational systems, training on improvised poetry was introduced in the public schools. Through the bertsolaritza's transmission board and following extensive self-reflection, teacher training initiatives, and program materials development, bertsolaritza classes are now offered in community outreach settings and the schools for general education. The project is active throughout the entire Basque Country, with 50 teachers in 465 schools providing educational opportunities to 28,000 students. Locally driven, bertso schools attract over 1,500 people per year. An additional 1,400 children and teenagers take part in extracurricular programs focused on bertsolarism. The bertsolaritza's original function to preserve and transmit the bertsolari's art to successive generations has been expanded by introducing social issues and recognizing the pleasure offered through the playful use of the Basque language. Bertsolari training is cross-disciplinary and therefore makes a meaningful contribution to the overall Basque educational system. Many well-known bertsolariak have been trained in the bertso schools, and thanks to this ambitious project, basic knowledge about bertsolarism has been disseminated across the entire Basque Country, as bertsolaris continue to expand and to improve that knowledge base.

Jone Uria focuses on one specific case, the improvisational poetry school of Algorta, one of the oldest bertso schools in the Basque Country, which celebrated its fortieth anniversary in 2020. This improvised poetry school, called Algortako Bertsolari Eskola (or ALBE), started as a meeting point for bertsozales (lovers of

Basque improvisational poetry) in Algorta (Bizkaia), as a place where people could sing bertsos and enjoy their shared passion for the craft. The Algorta school has now evolved into one of the most structured bertso schools, providing a space where children and young people begin their study of bertso technique and performance, and where experienced adults can practice and improve their skills. In collaboration with other regional groups, the school plays an essential role in organizing bertso-saioak (improvisational poetry gatherings) in Algorta and the Uribe Kosta region. In this paper, the author explains the self-organized nature of ALBE, assesses its impact on the area and the bertso community, and identifies some possible keys for success in a bertso-eskola.

In the research carried out on the bertso school of Bernat Etxepare High School in Baiona (Lapurdi), Miren Artetxe analyzes the relationship between the linguistic behaviors of the young people and the construction of their youth identities. In a sociolinguistic environment in which being competent in Basque is a marked characteristic among young people, the participants of the bertso schools have the habit of using Basque, not only in the bertso schools, but also among their friends. By analyzing the bertso schools as a community of practice, it has been possible to explore, at the same time, the relationship between group characteristics and individual identities, and the relationship of non-linguistic practices with linguistic practices. From the interviews carried out with fourteen young people and the related ethnographic work, some significant characteristics of the community of practice are pointed out, and Artetxe argues that through these characteristics, the members of the bertso schools develop a way of being young in Basque.

Julio Soto's paper answers a variety of questions, starting with how he came to the world of bertsolaritza, living in Iruñea in the 1990s in an environment with no connection to Basque improvisational poetry. What made this possible? What was the status of Navarrese improvisational poetry two decades ago? How strong was the bertsolaritza program in state-regulated education? And in the poetry schools? Finally, what is the current situation in Navarre?

Soto defends that the Basque improvisational poetry schools can become schools of life, as the education is equally important for both student and teacher: both gain an enhanced awareness of and appreciation for this invaluable part of Basque cultural heritage. He also explains his approach to teaching and building relationships at poetry school. And he analyzes the ways in which teaching has changed in the last few years and what this has meant for the evolution of bertsolaritza.

Starting with her personal experience, Maialen Lujanbio, bertsolari and first female winner of the bertsolari national championship, reflects on the impact of bertso schools in the practice of bertsolaritza. The creation of the bertso schools responded to deep social concerns and an awareness of the loss of Basque speakers and the potential loss of bertsolaritza. Throughout the twentieth century, the transmission and preservation of bertsolaritza largely occurred in rural areas, especially in farmhouses and taverns. In private spaces, improvisational poets were often asked to compose very particular types of poems. In public spaces, they generally performed in a setting that approximated a group's experience around a table after a meal. Most practitioners were men. As a result of urbanization and the weakening of oral traditions, bertsolaritza was under serious threat. However, the practice still thrives today as a living phenomenon that attracts youth, both in contemporary, urban areas and more traditional, rural settings. How did bertsolaritza, against all odds, become one of the most robust and most relevant cultural practices in the Basque Country? According to Lujanbio, the first and most important key to understanding this phenomenon is the creation of bertso schools and the new, "natural" way of transmitting the art they provided.

In his paper, artist and researcher Beñat Romera del Cerro reflects on the pedagogy of bertsogintza (the act of improvising poetry) within a constantly evolving landscape, and the practicing artist as a research object. The bertsolariak, from their unique creative perspectives, are continually creating new operating types through their experimentation. For that reason, the bertsolaritza must be a bridge between the personal creative laboratories of the bertsolari and everyday life, and they must also be open to transformation (in addition to being agents for transformation). Romera del Cerro suggests that the challenge of new educational proposals must be constantly tackled, precisely because improvisation can renew and change what is known, and he offers new artistic perspectives for the contemporary education of bertsogintza.

Finally, Larraitz Ariznabarreta, from the Center for Basque Studies, in the epilogue to this work, delves into the institutionalization of bertsolaritza as a contributor to its modernization, looks at the tensions that different ideological impulses in this institutionalization have created, and suggests questions for further research.

In the appendix, Reyes Lázaro and Jacqueline Urla interview Miren Artetxe and Maialen Lujanbio, providing a personal of about the evolution of bertsolaritza and their experience as women bertsolari.

The pandemic brought new challenges for academics, bertsolaritza and bertso schools. Social distancing is just the opposite of what any of them are about. Fortunately, scholars, bertsolariak, and bertsozaleak took advantage of new opportunities provided by remote resources, online conferencing, and video meetings. How is this going to impact the creative and learning processes? That is a question for a future conference, where we hope to be able to meet anyone interested in Basque improvised poetry. Once the world recovers from this long-lasting health crisis, we will reconvene and gather again around our tables, our papers, and our voices. When that time comes, the present book will be one of those on the table as we discuss bertsolaritza.

Larraitz Ariznabarreta
Iñaki Arrieta Baro
Xabier Irujo

Bertsolaritza: Beyond Transmission and Preservation

Oihana Iguaran Barandiaran

Oihana Iguaran holds a BA in audiovisual communications. Her research is focused on the interconnections between bertsolaritza and the media. She has been interested in bertsolaritza since childhood when she started to attend a bertso-eskola. She is a member of the Harituz Bertsozale Taldea and the Bertsozale Elkartea's Commission of Cultural Transmission.

Abstract

Bertsolarism (bertsolaritza) is an oral tradition passed on through generations. However, its transmission cannot be taken for granted. Bertsozale Elkartea (Association of Friends of Bertsolaritza) was created in 1985 with the primary aim of preserving this oral tradition. Hoping to counter the widespread belief that a bertsolari's talent is innate, many bertso-eskolak (bertsolarism schools) were set up in different towns and, in partnership with local educational systems, bertsolari training was introduced in the public schools. Through the bertso-eskolak's transmission board, and following extensive self-reflection, teacher training initiatives, and program materials development, bertsolaritza classes are now offered in community outreach settings, bertso-eskolak, and schools. The project is active throughout the entire Basque Country, with 50 teachers in 465 schools offering educational opportunities to 28,000 students. Locally driven, bertso-eskolak attract over 1,500 people per year. An additional 1,400 children and teenagers take part in extracurricular programs focused on bertsolarism. The bertso-eskolak's original mission to preserve and transmit the bertsolari's art to successive generations has been expanded through both the introduction of serious social issues and the recognition of the pleasure offered through the playful use of the Basque language. Bertsolari training is cross-disciplinary and therefore makes a meaningful contribution to the overall Basque educational system. Many well-known bertsolaris have been trained in the bertso-eskolak, and thanks to this ambitious project, basic knowledge about bertsolarism has been disseminated across the entire Basque Country. Bertsolaris continue to expand and to improve that knowledge base.

- "Is a bertsolari 'born' or 'made'?
At least the first time, he/she was born."
Joxe Agirre Oranda

To be a bertsolari: An innate or a learned trait? That is the initial question of interest for the bertsolaritza transmission committee. It is a debate not only concerning bertsolaritza; practitioners of other types of oral improvisation, too, have had to (or are still attempting to) untie that knot. Fortunately, many bertsolaris and bertsolaritza enthusiasts set out to prove the revolutionary hypothesis that bertsolaritza could indeed be learned, thus making the current educational movement possible. And, given the success of bertsolaritza today, many will join our companion Naroa Torralba, teacher at ALBE, in saying: "Bertso schools may have saved bertsolaritza."

Internationally, we are seeing similar models, whether they call themselves schools or work groups. Gloss schools, or "spontaneity workshops," where improvised poetry is taught, are held in various South American countries and are especially structured in a particularly specific way in Cuba. The didactic method for learning to improvise, included in the book Método Pimienta, also ponders the same question as its starting point: are improvisors born or made? The book provides Mexican troubadour Guillermo Velázquez's answer: "The improviser invents him or herself from birth . . ." (Pimienta 2014, 13).

It is one thing to say bertsolaritza can be learned, and another to actually learn it. Bertsolari and writer Xabier Amuriza was the first to describe how this learning process might look, and he gradually and progressively adapted it to bertsolaritza (Zu ere bertsolari [You Too Bertsolari]; Amuriza, 1982). At a very early stage, Joanito Dorronsoro also began to organize learning material that could be useful, for instance the Bertsotan 1789–1936 and Bertsotan II 1936–1980 anthologies, and Bertsotan: irakaslearentzako gidaliburua [Bertsotan: Teacher's Guide]. It was from these original criteria and instincts that bertsolaritza was taught and passed on in bertso schools.

The first bertso school was founded in 1974. As Pako Aristi claims in Antxoka Agirre's 2019 doctoral dissertation which describes the last 200 years of bertsolaritza transmission: "They began to teach bertsolaritza at a time when there were no bertso schools anywhere" (2019, 436). In fact, as Estitxu Eizagirre's blog about bertso schools underlines, transmission at bertso schools began "before Xabier Amuriza started to make his theorizations known," although the founders would later say that they had been aware of Amuriza's proposal. The first adult bertso school was set up in Santutxu, Bizkaia. In his dissertation, Agirre quotes Alberto Barandiaran: "There, in Santutxu, they immediately saw that bertso schools were interesting, autonomous tools for deepening Basque culture" (Agirre 2019, 440). Indeed, the goal of taking bertsolaritza into the future has served more than one purpose from the very beginning.

Like most oral traditions, bertsolaritza has been passed on from generation to generation—through old bertsos, memorized impromptu bertsos, or bertso papers. The live bertso sessions, and public spaces in general, have always been a place for natural transmission, as many people enjoy these experiences. The Bertsozale Elkartea's transmission committee keeps that very much in mind, and therefore their project includes live experiences for students, such as end-of-year festivals. At the same time, tournaments have a tremendous impact on the transmission of melodies, ideas, and patterns.

Although these natural places of transmission are now in good health, there was a serious concern about their continuity in the post-Franco era. As Pello Esnal described in his article, "Bat-bateko bertsogintzaren didaktika" (The Didactics of Spontaneous Bertsolaritza): "Basque society has been the best and almost the only bertso school to date" (1993). As Antton Aranburu and Joxe Mari Iriondo mentioned in their article, "Bertsolaritza gaur eta bihar" (Bertsolaritza Today and Tomorrow), the environment is what makes it possible to become a bertsolari: Bertsolaris come from the atmosphere rather than from their genetics. That atmosphere, however, was very difficult to achieve in the post-Franco era.

There were two opposing tendencies in the discussion:

> According to one attitude, bertsolaritza is something quite mythical. It is, in itself, a hidden gift of God, which is as fascinating as it is mysterious. Another attitude suggests there is no mystery; bertsolaritza has some techniques that could be learned from an early age, just like with any other subject. (. . .) If bertsolaris go to school, however, they must develop a theoretical basis for what they do. (Dorronsoro 1987, 24)

Had it not been for the intense concern for the perpetuation of bertsolaritza, this mystery may have never been solved; but necessity opened the door to the idea of schools and theorizing. If indeed bertsolaritza could be taught, how would one go about it? Pello Esnal tried to answer this question in his article: "Bertsolaritza apprentices have largely become [skilled] bertsolaris unconsciously, . . . and in some cases, awareness about this ability only came later" (1993, 104). Throughout Esnal's article, it is clear that in order to speak about the "didactics of bertsolaritza" it is necessary to deal with the "didactics of language." In other words, the shortcomings of the initial atmosphere in which bertsolaris were learning—those being a lack of limberness with the language and the topics themselves—meant that bertso schools were a necessity: "Today formal schools fill the gap created in those first [informal] schools" (Esnal 1993, 114).

Structuring

In order to launch formal schools, it was necessary to structure and organize an initially local movement. It was a revolutionary idea in its time. As Joanito Dorronsoro put it, "the most notable novelty" was bertso schools, "and the ways of doing things and infrastructures which had to be used in them" (1987, 23).

It is no coincidence that the original organizations which constituted the nuclei of the Bertsozale Elkartea (Association of Friends of Bertsolaritza), were created in response to the need to give structure to bertso schools: in the Northern Basque Country, Bertsularien Lagunak Elkartea (Friends of Bertsulari Association) was founded in 1980 and Nafarroako Bertsozale Elkartea (Navarrese Bertsolaris Association) followed in 1984. Schools were also organized in Araba from 1982 onwards, but there the Association was not formally set up until 1993. The bertsozale associations of Gipuzkoa and Bizkaia were also formed in 1993. In the meantime, an overarching bertsolari association was set up in 1986 through the organization of the national bertsolaritza tournament, which a year later broadened the focus of its mission and became the official Association of Friends of Bertsolaritza. Today, all these non-profit associations work with the aim of preserving, promoting, researching, and guaranteeing the future of bertsolaritza throughout the Basque-speaking country. There are currently a total of 2,500 members, 100 volunteers, and 70 professionals. These associations' work is organized into several departments: transmission, promotion, research, gender, communication, and dissemination.

This chapter will focus on the work carried out by the transmission committee. While the survival of bertsolaritza has been in the hands of all departments, the transmission committee has structured and promoted education about bertsolaritza.

Initially, Mikel Mendizabal and Antton Kazabon, members of the transmission committee, initially took charge of teaching material, basing their work on Amuriza's progressive, gradual model. Later, upon drawing up the curriculum, although Amuriza's work was taken as its basis, his progressive model was not taken into account and, partly because of that, paper (and the written word) took on a greater role in the methodology. The effort to return from using paper to orality will be discussed later in this chapter.

Current project dimension

The whole of the Bertsozale Elkartea is responsible for preserving bertsolaritza for future generations. With regards to the transmission committee specifically, this preservation involves "regenerating the whole ecosystem" that feeds bertsolaritza. Making bertsolaritza better known, attracting people to it, and giving everyone—not just bertsolaris—a space to be part of the project, are all goals. It could be said that the committee works in layers that feed one another, as shown in figure 1.1.

The project which reaches the largest number of people is official education (28,454 students at 463 schools during the 2019/2020 academic year), as it provides general information on bertsolaritza to students in schools throughout the Basque Country. Children who become enthusiastic about it can take bertso classes outside school hours, at bertso-eskolak, and many of them also take part in leisure time projects and become involved and active in the bertsolaritza movement (as we will see below, many of these students later become teachers).

It could be said, then, that the chain of transmission is organized in layers, and it most often starts from the broadest, most generalist area of official education. However, school classes are not the only point of access to bertso school. As can be seen in figure 1.1., some students attend bertso school directly, without any official school influence. Nonetheless, we will use the most common path taken by students (first official education, then bertso schools, then leisure time bertso activities)

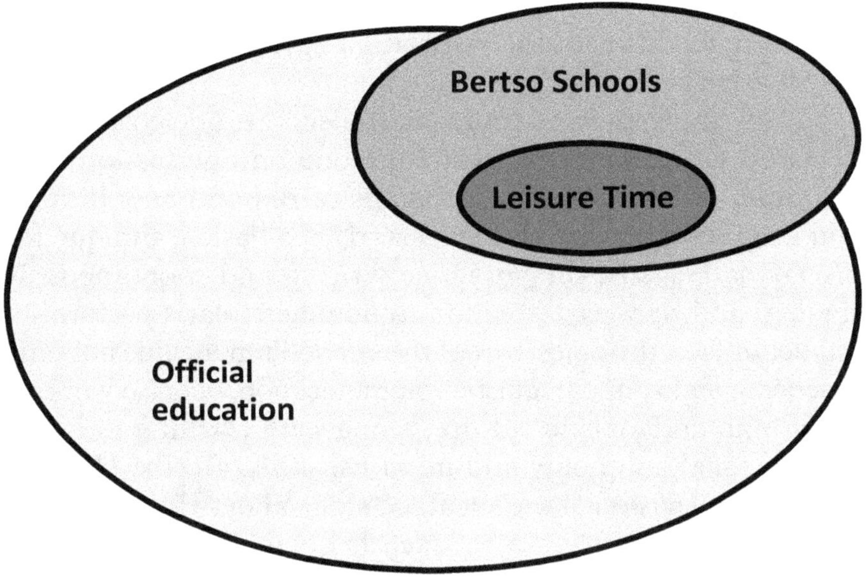

Figure 1.1. Graph of the Transmission Committee's projects as layers that feed each other

as our model to explain the current state of the project. In other words, we will explore the path from the first general contact with bertsolaritza to a deeper involvement and knowledge.

Official education

Bertsozale Elkartea's aim to preserve bertsolaritza, and one of the basic projects of the whole association, involves teaching bertsolaritza in schools. The goal is, in the committee's words, to "guarantee the basic transmission of bertsolaritza, and provide a methodological means for schools to work on different areas."[1] The initiative was launched in Navarre in 1985 in response to a request from schools. Later, as the project developed, it spread "to the whole Basque language area."[2] In the 2019–2020 school year, many children and young people in the Basque Country had the opportunity to practice bertsolaritza during school hours;

1 Ibid.
2 Ibid.

in fact, there were 28,454 students in 463 schools practicing the craft. To this end, the association currently has a team of fifty teachers offering continual training.

In this basic study program, students are offered authentic oral and written models: watching one-on-one sessions, for example, or listening to recordings of old and new bertsos and singing in groups. Students study the basic technique for preparing bertsos; they practice writing and spontaneously singing; and they pay attention to how bertsolaris perform in public. In fact, the objectives of the curriculum include not only practicing orality and linguistic communication, but also working on human and artistic culture, along with learning to learn, and personal autonomy and initiative skills. On the Hitzetik Hortzera television show's feature story about the classroom experience, Idoia Anzorandia, a teacher in the official education project, mentioned "Basque language" and "music" as core skills developed by the curriculum, but she believes other skills are developed simultaneously—"understanding other people's backgrounds and opinions, dealing with shyness, increasing self-esteem, teamwork, active listening[3] Students have opportunities to test in public what has been worked on during the course, thus gaining experience in real communicative situations. Some examples are taking part in local traditions, singing bertsos at school events (on Basque Language Day, during Carnival, etc.), or offering parents a show at the end of the school year (such as a bertso play or bertso rap).

'Bertsolaritza Curriculum' (Bertsolaritzaren Curriculuma Lehen Hezkuntzan 2008) is the pedagogical basis for teaching materials in use in official education. The creation of these materials always takes into account the Association's guidelines and care is taken to ensure that those with special needs can participate. It is worth mentioning that this study material received the Ixaka Lopez Mendizabal Award from the Basque Autonomous Community's Department of Education in 2011.

3 Watch here: https://www.eitb.eus/eu/get/multimedia/screenview/id/6770886/tipo/videos/telebista/

Aside from working with the material, students also create their own work each year, and their impromptu sessions are recorded as models and motivational sessions. Several departments at Bertsozale Elkartea, guided by material writers, coordinate in order to complete the material: teachers create content at a seminar; Lanku does the design; Xenpelar Documentation Center provides archival resources and biographies; all the sessions recorded by the dissemination committee are made available; and needs for material are adapted in line with research. The result of this collaboration has been the 2016 publication of Mundu bat bertso (A Bertso World) along with bertsoikasgela.eus.[4]

Although this material makes a major contribution on a daily basis, the team of fifty teachers is constantly researching and creating new material. Each year new work is carried out in line with our training and didactics framework. At the moment, for example, in connection with reflection about the methodology used, improvisation worksheets for the next ten years are being drawn up, along with a game box and classroom group activities. The latest challenge that the transmission committee has taken on is reflective training, as we will explain below.

In an educational model primarily based on writing, work on orality is a distinctive characteristic. In their book, The Art of Bertsolaritza (2001, 44–45) Joxerra Garzia, Jon Sarasua, and Andoni Egaña emphasized the "potential of the contribution of bertsolaritza to school education." The aim of their work was, in fact, "to show improvised bertsolaritza as being a specific and differentiated oral genre of literature" (Garzia, Sarasua, and Egaña 2001, 29). They saw many advantages to practicing bertso in the classroom—such as re-establishing a connection to improvisation, establishing contact with cultural heritage, and sharpening language and memory—and listed the following communication skills that would otherwise be difficult to develop: "Experience in and management of feedback; awareness of the conditioning factors of the surroundings [...] the entertainment

4 Website created to promote bertsolaritza in schools (2018): www.bertsoikasgela.eus

aspect: humor, irony, satire, etc.; strategies for impact on the sensibility of the listener" (Garzia, Sarasua, and Egaña 2001, 45–46). Mikel Artola, a teacher and researcher in the field, has drawn a similar conclusion almost twenty years later: "I would say that our project surmounts at least part of the difficulties encountered by official education in the transmission of culture."[5]

Therefore, that the project does more than spread basic knowledge of (and if possible, interest in) bertsolaritza, since another of its aims is to develop a positive attitude towards the Basque language and to develop public performance skills. These objectives, however, are goals merely aimed at students; practice has shown that the presence of improvisation in schools can also promote bertsolaritza in the general population and have a positive impact on the use of Basque language at a local level. It is no coincidence that some of the things most valued by town councils and schools involved in the project are "the dynamic methodology; practicing the language in an engaging, playful way that students enjoy; the closeness that teachers have with the children; humor; and the value that bertso-related performances add to school festivities and activities."[6]

If you ask teachers who work on the front lines day in and day out, they are clear about what the transmission project can offer students. Teacher Xan Alkhat, who works in the Northern Basque Country, mentions "an opening to the Basque world" and "a raising of consciousness";[7] teacher Idoia Anzorandia says that "we bring them a cultural framework that they are not familiar with";[8] and teacher and actor Oihane Perea, in a conversation on December 19, 2019, goes further, when speaking of the experience she has accumulated over the years:

> It (is) a place to create and enjoy in the Basque language. A greenhouse for the transmission of culture, a straightforward place in which to cultivate your

5 Interview with teacher and researcher Mikel Artola (January 13, 2020).
6 Evaluation from the transmission committee's annual 2018/2019 report
7 Interview with teacher Xan Alkhat, December 26, 2019.
8 Hitzetik Hortzera TV show, in it a section dedicated to classroom work (see footnote 9).

identity and creativity, a down-to-earth discipline. In this globalized, grey society, a strong foundation for local development, for color. Starting from joy-for-life rather than militancy.

"Enjoyment" is another word that teachers continually mention, and many consider it to be the key to success, as students learn without realizing while they are playing. This is what the Navarrese teacher Iker Gorosterrazu points out in a recent video report by the Government of Navarre: "The space for creativity in schools is quite limited, and [bertso is] a place for them to create, to create for the public, and it's usually an exercise and activity that they enjoy."[9] Perea, also, believes that "creating in Basque language gives [students] great pleasure."[10] According to this teacher and stakeholder from Araba, "It is a format that is adaptable and comfortable for them, and it serves to perform some functions that are important to them, things such as humor, complaints, expressing feelings, playing with words."[11] And despite realizing that they are working, as Alkhat says, "they feel that they are working in Basque and not being forced to work on bertsos."[12] It is something students achieve unexpectedly, as teacher and researcher Artola sees it: "If they get the playfulness of bertsos, they try to do it well without even realizing that they're doing it."[13]

Teacher Asier Alcedo, who works on the left bank of the Nerbioi River and the Enkartazioak area of Bizkaia, sums this experience up with a couple of anecdotes, remembering when five students from Barakaldo managed to sign up for the summer camps, and how on the fifth day one of them approached him and said, " 'Asier, I'm thinking in Basque!' And in those moments you realize that you are not just teaching how to put together rhymes, syllables, bertsos. You realize that you are doing slow,

9 See video: https://www.youtube.com/watch?v=TGH8Upx08OA&feature=youtu.be
10 Interview with teacher and agent Oihane Perea, December 19, 2019.
11 Idem.
12 Interview with teacher Xan Alkhat, December 26, 2019.
13 Interview with teacher and researcher Mikel Artola, January 13, 2020.

deep work."[14] Artola sees another objective that the project indirectly meets: "Sometimes bertsolaritza class becomes one of the only moments when children living in Spanish only speak Basque."[15] In the same way, the Bizcayan teacher Josu Landeta sums up the jump from the beginning to the end of the course in a single sentence: "Students go from not knowing anything about bertsos to producing something."[16] The song written by one of the bertso students for the school project describes what happens:

> Meter in your head and ideas dangling.
> I am freer in singing
> giving imagination a hand;
> I'm ready to take on the world.[17]

Students are not the only ones who enjoy the process; the teachers are indeed the true aficionados who have set their minds into the transmission of the craft. As Perea posits, "The bertso world makes you fall in love and become a part of it; passing that on to others and making a contribution to that world is a great source of satisfaction."[18] Alkhat also thinks himself lucky: "It's a great chance to have fun with children and the Basque language."[19] Teacher and researcher Mikel Artola sees those teachers' feelings as an added value "because we are teachers who love bertsolaritza and live it." They don't have to be improvisers themselves, but they do have to be "passionate fans"; as a result, Artola believes that "what we transmit is, above all, that passion, and the education system, at least in terms of culture, has problems with [a lack of] that."

Teachers share that enthusiasm, and that is what they have to get across to students. They are not blinded by nice moments, though; they are constantly looking for gaps and thinking about how to fill them. "We don't take different [Basque Language]

14 Interview with teacher Asier Alcedo, December 29, 2019.
15 Interview with teacher and researcher Mikel Artola, January 13, 2020.
16 Interview with teacher Josu Landeta, December 30, 2019.
17 Song and video: https://bertsoikasgela.eus/baliabideak/218/
18 Interview with teacher and agent Oihane Perea, December 19, 2019.
19 Interview with teacher Xan Alkhat, December 26, 2019.

dialects much into account,"[20] which Alkhat sees as something to be improved upon. "When it comes to teaching bertsos in sociologically immigrant and poorer areas, I feel like I'm out of place in some classrooms, or that I'm going to suggest things that don't suit some situations," says Alcedo with concern.[21] Landeta, on the other hand, believes that although the fact that groups are more and more heterogeneous (both in terms of their origins and their Basque language knowledge) makes the work more difficult, he "improves in ability to overcome obstacles" as he adapts the material, and he believes that "all students will have a bertso experience" during the school year.[22]

Bertso schools

Anyone who wants to advance past the basics learned in official education will be able to find a bertso school either in their own town or somewhere nearby. As the bertso schools map shows, currently 259 groups meet all over the Basque Country.[23] In those groups, students can continue to develop their knowledge, train as bertsolaris, and learn more about the bertsolaritza movement. As Harkaitz Zubiri pointed out at the Europa Bat-batean (Spontaneous Europe) academic conference: "Rather than training the bertsolaris of the future, what bertso schools do most is create a critical mass for bertsolaritza and produce networks of friendship which fulfil this role."[24]

Bertso schools have different aims. Some meet to train bertsolaris, others aim to promote the Basque language, others seek to share their bertso enthusiasm. The result, however, usually brings many of these goals together. Often the local bertso schools give sustenance to the whole local bertsolaritza

20 Idem.
21 Interview with teacher Asier Alcedo, December 29, 2019.
22 Interview with teacher Josu Landeta, December 30, 2019.
23 The bertso schools map is available: https://bdb.bertsozale.eus/web/mapa/bertso-eskolak
24 Zubiri, Harkaitz 2016. "Kultur ekosistema sortzeko estrategia, bertsolaritza garaikidean transmisioa ulertzeko gako" ("Strategy for creating a cultural ecosystem, a key to understanding transmission in contemporary Bertsolaritza"). *Europa bat-batean. International Improvised Singing Meeting.* Academic Conferences. Donostia, July 2016.

movement, as Jon Sarasua says, and Antxoka Agirre quotes in his thesis:

> Bertsolaris are the basic nuclei of the bertsolaritza movement. Bertso schools are not schools in an academic sense, simply teaching to pass things on; more than that they are workshops, groups, sometimes small associations, that carry out bertsolaritza's local tasks: transmission, also promotion, and perhaps the collection of material, along with self-organizing (. . .). The roles which the association carries nationwide, in fact. (Agirre 2019, 627)

In other words, far from behaving like mere local transmission committees, bertso schools often act in terms of the perspectives of all the committees which work in favor of the survival of bertsolaritza. Being aware of their autonomy and independence as a movement, the association does provide them with as many resources and as much support as it can.

According to data for the 2109/2020 academic year, there are 259 bertso schools in operation throughout the Basque Country, with 1,796 people taking part in them (see figures 1.2 and 1.3 for province-by-province numbers).

Typically, each group meets up with a teacher (238 teams out of 259 do this, while the other 21 groups carry out that role by teaching each other). There are a total of 112 teachers at bertso schools in the Basque Country. Most of the groups (192 out of 259) are composed of underage students who are just starting out or improving their improvisational skills. There are 57 adult-only groups, and in the remaining ten groups both adults and underage students take part.

What all bertso schools share is their love of bertsolaritza, and that enthusiasm can take many forms. For example, only a small number of groups are at ease when improvising (29), the majority of groups work on improvisation skills (125), and there are many newcomers (87). There are, however, a few groups that come together specifically to train for the tournament (6),

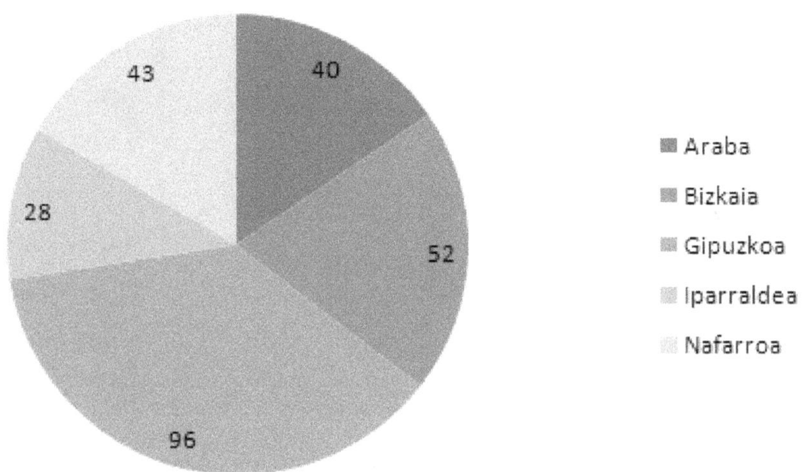

Figure 1.2: Bertso school groups by province.

a couple of groups which meet simply to enjoy bertsolaritza and organize sessions, and some which place themselves outside of any of those classifications (10).

This classification of types of bertso schools is not definitive. As mentioned above, bertsolaris who come together in groups have varying goals. Some of these bertso schools (ALBE, Harituz, Bortzirietako Bertso Eskola, Lilibertso, etc.)[25] are organized by geographical area or group, giving sustenance to the whole bertsolaritza movement in their community throughout the year, by, for example, organizing competitions, sessions, and other events connected with bertsolaritza. In short, as Jon Sarasua said in his article about local initiatives, "the way to carry out bertsolaritza at the grassroots level is the group" (Sarasua 1993, 37), and he adds, "Bertsolaritza groups get together, train, enjoy,

25 Further explanation about specific groups: ALBE: Algorta Bertso School, whose initiatives can be followed on its website (http://www.albe.eus/). Harituz: Tolosaldeko Bertsozaleen Elkargunea (Tolosa area bertsolaritza enthusiasts' association), is a promoter of the local bertsolaritza movement. Bortzirietako Bertso Eskola (Bortzirieta Bertso School): It includes Lesaka and Igantzi Bertso Schools. Lilibertso: A group of bertsolaris from Gernika and the surrounding area; it is very active on social networks (for example, https://www.facebook.com/lilibertso/).

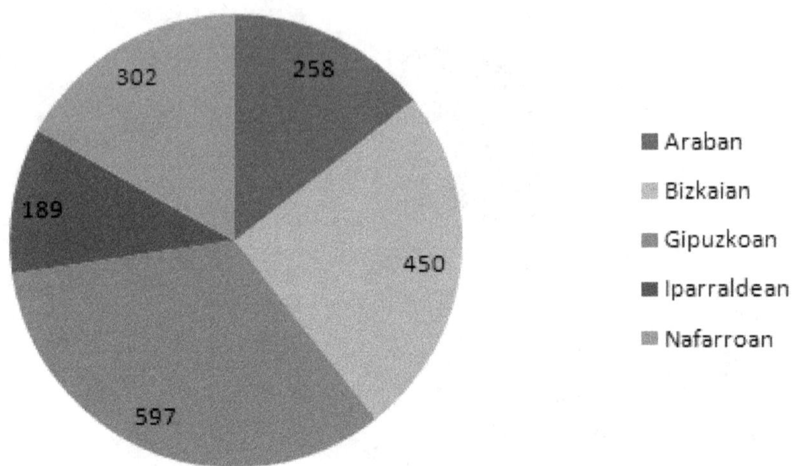

Figure 1.3: Bertso school participants by province.

and, in addition to taking initiatives, take it upon themselves to teach others" (1993, 42). He concludes that this activity in local areas is "grassroots bertsolaritza," (1993, 40) which is why he does not see the work of bertso schools as "creating an elite, but rather, the inherent sense of bertsolaritza" (1993, 40).

Bertso schools being what Sarasua calls "grassroots bertsolaritza," there are still concerns about gender issues, with data showing that gender distribution at bertso schools among underage members is 55% male to 45% female. This gap widens among adults, with 30% women and 70% men (one person in the survey identified as non-binary). Looking at this data, one might think that it will be a matter of time for the numbers to balance out among young people. Currently, however, there is a different trend.

According to the latest sociological study carried out by Bertsozale Elkartea, and as summarized in researchers' Harkaitz Zubiri, Xabier Aierdi, and Alfredo Retortillo's book Kultura ez da bat-batekoa. Bertsolaritza aztergai (Culture is not spontaneous. An examination of bertsolaritza), the gender

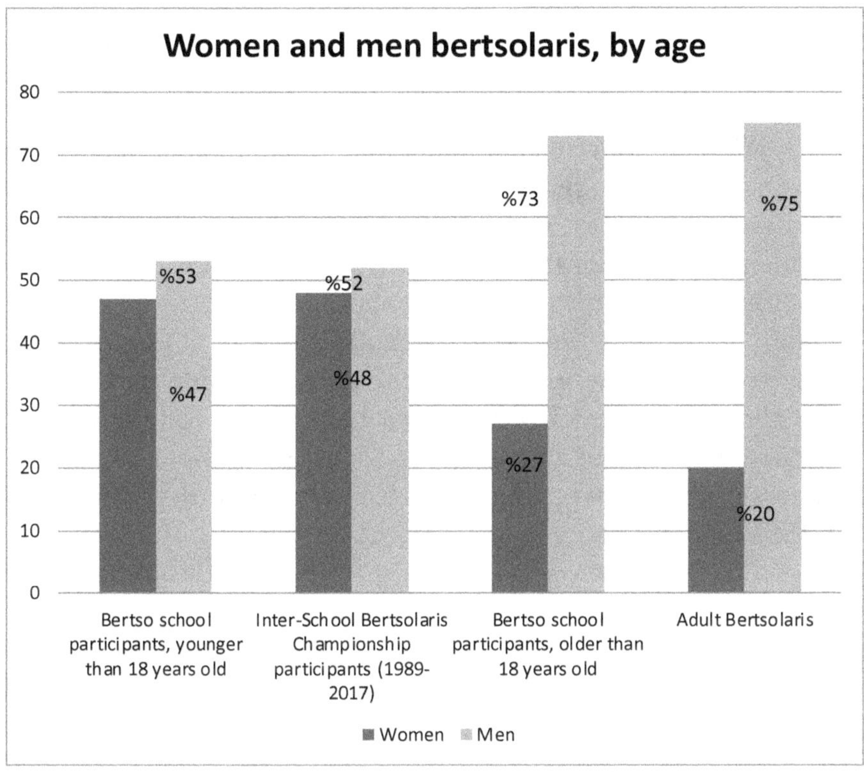

Figure 1.4: Data published in the latest sociological study by Harkaitz Zubiri (Zubiri 2019, 147)

glass ceiling in bertsolaritza is still very much present. But there is hope for bertso schools:

> Bertsolaritza schools have created better conditions for girls to be part of bertsolaritza. In fact, more than places for transmission, bertso schools are spaces for socialization as Miren Artetxe (2014), Ainhoa Agirreazaldegi, and Arkaitz Goikoetxea (2007) have well explained. (. . .) This context is more comfortable than the world of bertsolaritza, and bertso schools are more welcoming in a wider ecosystem. (. . .)

> A new generation is growing up in bertso schools, and this could lead to the next great transformation in bertsolaritza. (Zubiri et al. 2019, 156)

We can conclude, therefore, from figure 1.4 and from Zubiri's own words, that bertso schools are trusted places where it is possible to work toward gender balance. The following statement, in reference to a qualitative study, is given by a man aged 30–45: "I think bertso schools are the starting point for [gender] improvements. Bertso schools are like a Trojan horse in the traditional world . . . Women travel inside this horse" (Zubiri et al. 2019, 156). In spite of that hope for the future, there are still obvious challenges ahead. For example, of the 112 teachers currently working at bertso schools, only 32 of them (or 28%) are women.

The Association organizes various activities to complete the traditionally autonomous organization of bertso schools: bertso school days, adult bertso school days (currently held in conjunction with Bertso Day), courses, and an inter-school bertsolari tournament (for under-eighteen-year-olds). Other initiatives launched by the Association are now being developed by bertso schools. For instance, Bertsotruk is a project for bertso schools to get to know each other in an organized, alternating fashion, which had previously been done spontaneously by some bertso schools and which several have now decided to continue being part of. Similarly, regarding courses, bertso schools have the opportunity to propose topics and can then request training, the cost of which the Association partly covers. During bertso school days there are large gatherings with many special sessions and performances for children and adults alike. Bertso school themselves also take part in the organization.

In terms of teaching material, the digital portal put together by Bertsozale Elkartea for bertso schools was opened in September 2019.[26] In addition to providing resources for enjoying and training for bertsolaritza, it also aims to encourage

26 https://bertsoeskola.eus/

networking between bertso schools, incorporating sites for publishing each other's work, for example. The portal provides information about bertso schools and is a source for following and studying current bertsolaritza. The material has been chosen carefully, considering all the Association's objectives and with an understanding of bertso schools in a broad sense. In addition to material for learning about bertsos (rhyme search, melody, compilations, etc.), the website offers instructions for organizing sessions and bertso competitions. Positive reception was immediate, according to data provided by the transmission department: in the first month there were more than 3,000 visits, with more than 1,400 people searching for local materials.

The longest-running project in connection with bertso schools is the Inter-School Bertsolaris Championship. The way it has developed is remarkable. The first championship was organized in 1989, 2019 marking its thirtieth anniversary in both Gipuzkoa and the whole of the Basque Country. Over the years, we have seen many young people from the bertso schools' first generation singing their first bertsos in public at the inter-school competition, and many of the bertsolaris who perform in public today won their first trophies at this competition. The aim of the inter-school competition is for young people attending bertso schools to "have the opportunity to perform spontaneously in public,"[27] and provide a site for children and young people to enjoy bertsos as listeners.

The way to approach the objectives has changed as experience is gained. In 2014, there was a reflection about inter-school competitions in conjunction with the bertso schools. The Ikastola (original Basque medium schools) Association also took part, as it had been organizing the inter-school tournament in collaboration with the Association for the last six years. An agreement was reached to hold non-competitive sessions for the youngest students. Juanito Dorronsoro wrote his concern about a similar issue a dozen years prior, in his book Zumaiako bertso eskola: 20 urte kantari (Zumaia Bertso School: 20 Years

27 https://www.bertsozale.eus/eu/eskolartekoa

of Singing): "In our competitive, capitalist society, might not putting children in tough competition with each from an early age be contrary to good pedagogical practice?" (2002, 46). Prior to 2014, fourteen-year-olds had participated in groups, and fifteen-to-eighteen-year-olds individually. During a group reflection it was decided that competing in public was not necessary and it was suggested that other types of sessions be held for children fourteen and under (bertso snacks, teaching sessions, public exercises prepared at bertso school, singing bertso-papers, etc.). Students fourteen years of age and under can still take part in inter-school bertso-paper competitions as they have always done.

Since 2014 the yearly bertso school tournament has, therefore, been aimed at young people aged fifteen to eighteen. Nowadays, in addition to participating as bertsolaris, they can take part in topic-setting, organizing, and other roles. Each province has its own festival, with qualifying rounds and a final. Two bertsolaris from each of the seven provinces qualify for the Basque Country's inter-school bertsolari competition. There is a full-day celebration around the fourteen young bertsolaris' session. In recent years, the network of young bertsolaris has become stronger both on and off stage, as many have known each other from bertsolaritza summer camps. This all turns into a celebration between friends on the final day.

Leisure Time Activities

Leisure time bertso activities are designed to be "an incentive for motivation, support for daily work, and a meeting place for young bertsolaris" who go to bertso school.[28] The most popular leisure projects are the bertso summer camps,[29] which have been growing and gaining strength since the first was held in Hazparne (in the Northern Basque Country) in 1998.

28 Section explaining the project on the Bertsozale Association site: http://www.bertso-eskolak.eus/orriak/get/16-Bertsolaritzan-transmisioa#ekintza%20osagarriak

29 Explanation about bertso summer camps: https://www.bertsozale.eus/eu/bertso-udalekuak-eta-barnetegiak

Nowadays, five rounds are held each year (taking into account the Association's criteria regarding geographical inclusion), and a total of 210 young people aged nine to eighteen take part. A team of forty educators also take part as supervisors, principals, and chefs. Many of those who are now educators began going to the summer camps as children, which demonstrates the extensive transmission cycle in leisure projects.

Before the Association started organizing bertso summer camps around the Basque Country, several bertso schools held residential courses, trying to offer young bertsolaris a space to get to know each other and share their enthusiasm. And, implicitly, bertso summer camps (and later all leisure projects) have also become a meeting place to enrich and enjoy what bertsolaritza entails: breathing and reinforcing the Basque language. With the participation of children from all over the Basque Country, the diversity of Basque dialects is very much present, and many young people become familiar with the variety of sounds in the Basque language for the first time at these camps. As educator Ane Labaka explains, "They also become aware of the Basque Country, and find another way to communicate through and with the Basque language."[30] Teacher and bertsolari Oihane Perea also talks about the community which carries out transmission work, emphasizing the leisure activities specifically: "All this is rounded off in leisure projects, the foundations are laid there, deepening personal and creative relationships that will be useful over the years."[31]

Labaka has been an educator at bertso camps for ten years (and the director of one for the last five years) and is clear that the most satisfying thing is the young bertsolaris' networking: "When I see them all friends, and all networked, I think this is one of the best things that can happen to bertsolaritza, and it is a sign of bertsolaritza's health going into the future."[32] Many of the networks created at summer camps continue on, and we have seen that this camaraderie deepens children and young

30 Interview with educator and founder Ane Labaka, January 13, 2020.
31 Interview with teacher and activist Oihane Perea, December 19, 2019.
32 Interview with educator and bertsolari Ane Labaka, January 13, 2020.

people's commitment to the project. Among the many songs and bertsos that are created at summer camps, this one was sung in 2019 in Orio: "We imagine the network that holds us up."[33] And not only do they imagine it, the young bertsolaris achieve it by sewing their networks together in the days they spend together. "[It is] a parallel world to some extent; and in this parallel world it is possible for creativity to take on a different place, for the Basque language to have a different degree of prestige," summer camp director Labaka points out.

Labaka sees this journey as a milestone, a time when participants begin to work on other values in addition to bertsolaritza: "Somehow we started to work on gender perspective, with the treatment of diversity and its importance, . . . I think that became central, and we try to work from that perspective." Beyond these values which affect a wider sphere than bertso, the enlargement of the way in which bertso is understood has led to the inclusion of other leisure projects, such as the Ahots Baten (In One Voice) residential creativity course.[34] Additionally, bertso offers a chance to get together and nurture other creative disciplines at the Mintzola Oral Workshop (organized in collaboration with the Ikastola Association). Since opening in 2015, every year for five days it brings together forty young people aged 15–23, along with five educators, and, in addition to bertsolaritza, participants practice theatre, literature, and singing with guest artists.

Given the good results obtained through leisure projects, and the high demand for them, another project, similar to the Ahots Baten creative residency, was launched in 2019 at the University of the Basque Country in collaboration with the Laboa Chair: Ahostegunak (Voice Thursdays).[35] Young people aged 18–22 were offered five sessions to have fun with "oral culture creation," each session lasting three hours. In this case

33 Video filmed in 2019 in Orio. Available along with other sessions and years: https://www.youtube.com/watch?v=ChFmC_7phxQ
34 Further information about the Ahots Baten project: https://www.mintzola.eus/eu/elkargunea/ahots-baten-sormen-egonaldia
35 More details about the 'Ahostegunak' project: https://www.mintzola.eus/eu/elkargunea/ahostegunak

in addition to bertso, they worked on literature, singing, and theatre.

A large number of children have learned about bertsolaritza at school (more than 28,000 students every year). As a result of the Association's leisure projects, those who liked it had the opportunity to train further outside of school and, at the same time, feel part of a group and experiment with different areas of bertsolaritza with friends who share their enthusiasm. They can take part in school bertsolari competitions (spontaneous writing), help organize sessions (be local activists to an extent), and continue developing this experience throughout the Basque Country, and intensively in the leisure programs they enjoy (which now also offer the opportunity to explore further creative disciplines).

Through these layers of transmission, basic knowledge of bertsolaritza is now widely spread, and the bertsolaritza movement regularly gains new accomplices and members. As Labaka says:

> I think that the summer camps develop that too and, in fact, it becomes a way to be part of the association, to be part of the bertso movement and, if volunteers are needed, to take part at bertso schools in sessions and tournaments (. . .) or to collect data for sociological analysis (. . .). There are people who leave the summer camps feeling themselves to be part of the movement, and people who have not gone to the summer camps who want to take part too. So, I would say that they are a starting point for them later joining the overall bertsolaritza movement. (January 13, 2020)

It could be said that while the whole Association plays an important role in "preserving bertsolaritza," the transmission committee has invented a way to nurture the general ecosystem that in turn nourishes the bertsolaritza movement. As the ecosystem changes, however, new ways of feeding it must be found, and the staff and volunteers on the committee are constantly working to ensure this, as the following section shows.

Towards reflective training

The recent review of the current situation of the transmission committee shows that most of the people in Bertsozale Elkartea's professional group are currently employed in the educational sector. The project has taken on a huge dimension, and the staff are self-demanding in their daily work. As a sign of this, according to the strategic reflection carried out by Bertsozale Elkartea in 2018, transmission and education grew in importance. From professional teachers in schools to teachers at bertso schools and summer camp educators, all practitioners work on issues that go beyond bertsolaritza. A proposal to change the name of the committee also arose, seeking terms that invoked education or similar ideas. In fact, the entire professional group influences education on a daily basis, and they felt the need to recognize and accept their responsibility toward that education in order to facilitate the project's response and position in terms of education.

Things were already changing in the committee, and in the 2017/2018 academic year, a process of reflection was launched—at the request of teachers—with the aim of reducing the gap between the project's aims and what was being achieved in practice. The stakeholders already felt the need to make changes to the training that teachers were receiving and, in parallel, to coordinate the digitalization of teaching material.

The point is, the curriculum should be a general framework for the project's contribution to culture, music, language, and personal-social skills. However, in order to achieve this, according to Mikel Artola, "our students must experience being a bertsolari and a listener." Experience has shown Artola that students who are nervous and trying to do well, are immersed in deep concentration, which guarantees this contribution: "Bertsolaris' experience of improvisation, and more so in public, is very powerful." Artola understands this experience as a process of empowerment, and believes that it "is at the heart of our project, and it involves more than just bertsolaritza, it is almost about life itself."

With methods drawn from the writing-based curriculum, it is questionable to what extent this experience Artola refers to is activated in the classroom. For example, Artola recalls that at the end of the course he asked students to define bertsolaritza from what they had learned, and that no one mentioned it was spontaneous. "This," he says, "does not happen if they try to improvise themselves." So one of the concerns raised by teachers is whether or not the method should lean toward more spontaneity, based on a bertsolari's real experience. In order to plan this well, however, Artola felt the "need for research," and he set out on a path that could be summarized as "from practice to becoming an expert." He thinks it is the right time and place: "What the Association does have is the instinct to integrate change."

The teachers' request was not the first call to focus on orality. By 1986, communication expert Joxerra Garzia had begun to emphasize the contribution that bertsolaritza could make to education. In his article "Bertsolaritza in school curriculum," he expressed his concern: "The neglect of orality in schools relates to the methods of transmitting knowledge: namely, the fact that the written word is still usurping the prime position" (1986, 70). Garzia saw a serious need to include orality in the curriculum: "The capacity for oral communication is a prerequisite if we want to succeed in today's society" (Garzia 1986, 73). If communication was shifting to oral communication in 1986, it could be said that this trend is on the increase; Garzia himself emphasized the same need at the 2011 Ahoa Bete Hots conference held by the Mintzola Oral Workshop.[36]

It was in that setting that Mikel Artola began his training and research.[37] He identified three problems: the didactic method,

36 The conference collection was published as a book, and is available online: https://www.mintzola.eus/eu/files/ahozko-elkargunea/ahoa-bete-hots-2011-liburua

37 The research which Mikel Artola is carrying out: Innovation in the Bertsolaritza Elkartea education project. Active research to influence teaching methods, teacher training, and the organization's culture.

teacher training, and the organization's culture—the so-called "pedagogical trio":

> An improvement that aims to have a positive impact on student learning, should affect all levels of the school, involving three major areas (a certain "pedagogical trio," as someone has called it): development of the school as organization, teacher training, and curriculum development. (Bolivar 2002, 49)

Bringing this pedagogical concept to the Bertsozale Elkartea would mean that the didactic method would first have to be revamped, because it is currently based on writing, and because the benefits mentioned in connection with spontaneous experience require more oral-based methods. Secondly, in terms of teacher training, replacing what has hitherto been a mistaken attempt at thoughtful training, with one that turns the teacher into a researcher—empowering him or her—would be required. And finally, the Association, aware of the fact that it is also an educational institution, should become an organization that participates in self-reflection. The aim is to make the Association a "professional learning community" (Krichesky and Murillo Tordecilla 2011).

So, innovation must be applied to the teaching of bertsolaritza (when limited to pen and paper, the student does not actually experience bertsolaritza); to the culture of the organization; and to teacher training. The main challenge is to establish improvised bertsolaritza as a regular learning unit. To do this, Albert Casals has been to mirror the oral experiences devised[38] (along with Aléxis Díaz Pimienta[39]), and the center's improvisation method has been trialed in several classrooms. Both teachers and students were satisfied with the experience. "The

38 Albert Casals wrote a thesis in 2009 on oral teaching of the Catalan improvisation tradition: "La cançó amb text improvisat: Disseny i experimentació d'una proposta interdisciplinària per a Primària." Available online: https://www.tdx.cat/handle/10803/4659

39 In 2014 Aléxix Díaz Pimienta published "Método Pimienta para la Enseñanza de la Improvisación Poética (Oralitura)" (Methodology for the Teaching of Poetic Improvisation) after organizing methods learned during improvisation courses.

teachers at the center tell us that we really started doing what we had been saying," Artola explains, emphasizing amazement at what students achieve with the new methodology.

Thanks to the good results of the pilot, this model of reflective training has been extended to all teachers, and they are currently working on the observation phase. In other words, teachers are becoming researchers and observers of their own daily work, recording classes on video so that they can then be reviewed in groups. Reflective training is cyclical and organized for the long run, but it has already led to a change in culture and methodology, which is proving to be beneficial.

Beyond bertsolaritza

The transmission committee's aim is to nourish the entire ecosystem that makes up the bertsolaritza movement. At first, local people self-organized to convey oral cultural heritage whose oral transmission was not guaranteed; the Association took on this role later. However, something more than perpetuating this heritage and passing it on to future generations has been achieved: by making this heritage a tool, it has also become a tool for achieving many other goals. The transmission committee has not only transmitted the craft of bertsolaritza, but also a whole way of being and acting. And that has turned transmission into a cycle.

In addition to local organizations and the network created by the Association, it should be mentioned that natural transmission has been reinforced: more than 1,600 sessions per year can be seen live in all areas of the Basque Country.[40] One can also enjoy these sessions online, which has become the strongest transmission site of all.[41] These online bertsolaritza sessions are widely used to work on improvisation individually, or in groups and at schools, to make specific choices and links to their own websites (bertsoeskola.eus and bertsoikasgela.eus).

40 Data provided by the Xenpelar Documentation Centre (2016 onwards).
41 Digital portal for following public activities: www.bertsoa.eus

The transmission committee has become a tool for nourishing itself. As teacher Alkhat puts it, "To see the children and young people, my former students, in bertso sessions (as bertsolaris, listeners, or assistants) is truly satisfying." Bertso schools have become a means for practicing Basque: "It causes a change in children's attitudes toward a language that was completely devalued and despised," according to teacher Alcedo. Eventually, it becomes the ecosystem itself that nourishes transmission. In addition to bertsolaritza:

> The bertso movement has been an active factor in the country's language recovery process. (. . .) It is an active agent in nation building and culture. Bertso schools have always been the breathing space for the Basque language in Araba. Teachers, Basque activists, Basque teachers, singers, Basque language technicians, journalists, presenters, writers, poets, have all come out of bertso schools. Bertsolaritza has also been nurtured and constantly revitalized. Community building takes place there. From one hand to the next. (Interview with Oihane Perea, December 19, 2019)

Community building, or team building, or network building, as young people have shown us; or even nation building: "the way to carry out bertsolaritza at the grassroots level is the group," said Sarasua (1993, 37). Perhaps the way to carry out bertsolaritza nationally is a network, a community, a group: a professional learning community, or a voluntary network, or a group of friends. Sarasua said that in order to work in favor of transmission, one had to "just close one's eyes." But we have also figured out how to widen and adjust our perspective. "We in the world of bertso are the result of conscious, intelligent transmission, and perhaps we now are (aren't we great!) agents of an even more intelligent form of transmission" (Sarasua 2014, 1). In 2020, the most wide-reaching, well-prepared team of bertsolaritza teachers ever was on the road to reflective training.

As teacher Alkhat says, "We may not do everything well, but the desire to do well also pays off."[42]

By signing bertsos we have learned that even what is not done well is valid. Part of the path is having thick feet, thin feet and not being afraid to get your feet wet. "In the beginning there was no school, and everything was school," Esnal (1993) wrote. Bertsolaritza offers you this school (or network, or community, or group); Maialen Lujanbio gave this invitation to sing on Bertso Day, 2019.[43]

> "Stand up to your fears
> and forget criticism
> come to bertso school
> fill your lungs
> deepen your reasons
> sharpen your provocation
> songs are needed by
> everyone's cravings
> scruffy and pretty,
> in rags and talking
> especially young people
> and every other one's a girl
> so the statistics
> can go crazy."

Appendix: teaching material

Aizpurua, Karlos, Altube, Amaia, Arozena, Estitxu, and Aurrekoetxea, Iñaki. *Bertsolaritzaren Curriculuma Lehen Hezkuntzan.* Oiartzun: Lanku eta Euskal Herriko Bertsozale Elkartea, 2008. https://bdb.bertsozale.eus/web/liburutegia/view/1698-Bertsolaritzan-curriculuma-lehen-hezkuntzan.

42 Interview with teacher Xan Alkhat, December 26, 2019.
43 The main Bertso Day festival was held on January 26, 2019, in Barañain, and it took "bertso school" as its topic. Maialen Lujanbio sang this bertso as her farewell. Video: https://bertsoa.eus/bertsoak/16185-bukaerako-agurra

Aizpurua, Mikel. *Bertsoz play: lehen hezkuntza : 4. maila.* Accessed January 26th, 2020. https://bdb.bertsozale.eus/web/liburutegia/view/1043-bertsoz-play-lehen-hezkuntza-4.-maila.

Bertsolaritzaren Curriculuma Lehen Hezkuntzan. Oiartzun ; Villabona: Lanku Bertso Zerbitzuak : Euskal Herriko Bertsozale Elkartea, 2008. https://bdb.bertsozale.eus/common/file/get/67609.

Aizpurua, Mikel, Kazabon, Antton, and Mendizabal, Mikel. *Bertsoz bai: 2. maila : bigarren hezkuntza.* Donostia: Ikastolen Elkartea, 2007. https://bdb.bertsozale.eus/web/liburutegia/view/1526-bertsoz-bai-2.-maila-bigarren-hezkuntza.

———. *Bertsoz bai: bigarren hezkuntza : 1. maila.* Donostia: Ikastolen Elkartea, 2006. https://bdb.bertsozale.eus/web/liburutegia/view/3850-bertsoz-bai-bigarren-hezkuntza-1.-maila.

———. *Bertsoz blai: 5. maila, lehen hezkuntza.* Donostia: Ikastolen Elkartea, 2004. https://bdb.bertsozale.eus/web/liburutegia/view/1590-bertsoz-blai-5.-maila-lehen-hezkuntza.

———. *Bertsoz blai: lehen hezkuntza : 6. maila.* Donostia: Ikastolen Elkartea, 2005. https://bdb.bertsozale.eus/web/liburutegia/view/1589-bertsoz-blai-lehen-hezkuntza-6.-maila.

———. *Bertsoz play: lehen hezkuntza: 3. maila.* Donostia: Ikastolen Elkartea, 2002. https://bdb.bertsozale.eus/web/liburutegia/view/4005-bertsoz-play-lehen-hezkuntza-3.-maila.

Amuriza, Xabier. *Bertsolaritza 1: hitzaren kirol nazionala.* Bilbao: AEK, 1981.

———. *Bertsolaritza 2: hiztegi errimatua.* Bilbao: AEK Bizkaieraz bertsotan. Bilbao: Bizkaia Bertsozale Elkartea, 1996.

———. *Bizkaierazko hiztegi errimatua*, 1996.

———. *Hiztegi errimatua.* Andoain: Lanku, 2016.

———. *Hiztegi errimatua: hitzaren kirol nazionala*. Bizkaia: Bizkaia Bertsozale Elkartea, 1997.

———. *Zu ere bertsolari*. AEK. Gráficas Lizarra SL: ELKAR, 1982.

Amuriza, Xabier, and Garzia, Joxerra. *Bertsoen mundua*. Accessed November 20th, 2019. https://bdb.bertsozale.eus/web/liburutegia/view/1732-bertsoen-mundua.

Dorronsoro, Joanito. *Bertsotan 1789-1936*. Donostia: Gipuzkoako Ikastolen Elkartea, 1981. https://bdb.bertsozale.eus/web/liburutegia/view/3258-bertsotan-1789-1936.

———. *Bertsotan II: 1936-1980*. Donostia: Gipuzkoako Ikastolen Elkartea, 1988.

———. *Bertsotan: irakaslearentzako gidaliburua*. Donostia: Gipuzkoako Ikastolen Elkartea, 1982.

Eizagirre, Ixiar. *Gu ere bertsotan, 1*. Oiartzun: Lanku, 2010. https://bdb.bertsozale.eus/web/liburutegia/view/1687-gu-ere-bertsotan-1.

Eizagirre, Ixiar, and Lagoma, Erika. *Gu ere bertsotan 2*. Oiartzun: Lanku, 2010. https://bdb.bertsozale.eus/web/liburutegia/view/1685-gu-ere-bertsotan-2.

Garzia, Joxerra, Garzia, Pako, Kazabon, Antton, and Mendizabal, Mikel. *Bertso ostatua: 7. maila*. Donostia: Gipuzkoako Ikastolen Elkartea eta Euskal Herriko Bertsolari Elkartea, 1989. https://bdb.bertsozale.eus/web/liburutegia/view/4135-bertso-ostatua-7.-maila.

———. *Bertso ostatua: 8. maila*. Donostia: Gipuzkoako Ikastolen Elkartea eta Euskal Herriko Bertsolari Elkartea, 1990. https://bdb.bertsozale.eus/web/liburutegia/view/4146-bertso-ostatua-8.-maila.

———. *Bertso-galaxia: 5. maila*. Donostia: Gipuzkoako Ikastolen Elkartea eta Euskal Herriko Bertsolari Elkartea, 1989. https://bdb.bertsozale.eus/web/liburutegia/view/4137-bertso-galaxia-5.-maila.

———. *Bertso-galaxia: 6. maila*. Donostia: Gipuzkoako Ikastolen Elkartea eta Euskal Herriko Bertsolari Elkartea, 1989. https://bdb.bertsozale.eus/web/liburutegia/view/4134-bertso-galaxia-6.-maila.

———. *Bertso-trena: 3. maila*. Donostia: Gipuzkoako Ikastole Association and Euskal Herriko Bertsolari Elkartea, 1988. https://bdb.bertsozale.eus/web/liburutegia/view/4133-bertso-trena-3.-maila.

———. *Bertso-trena: 4. maila*. Donostia: Gipuzkoako Ikastolen Elkartea eta Euskal Herriko Bertsolari Elkartea, 1988. https://bdb.bertsozale.eus/web/liburutegia/view/4136-bertso-trena-4.-maila.

Kazabon, Antton. *Letrak bertsotan O.H.O 1. maila*. Donostia: ELKAR, 1987. https://bdb.bertsozale.eus/web/liburutegia/view/1307-letrak-bertsotan-oho-1.-maila.

Kazabon, Antton, and Mendizabal, Mikel. *Txikitik Handira*. Donostia: Gipuzkoako Ikastolen Elkartea, 1993. https://bdb.bertsozale.eus/web/liburutegia/view/1323-txikitik-handira.

Mendizabal, Mikel, Irastorza, Sabino, and Kazabon, Antton. *Ahozkotasuna: I. hezkuntzan*. Donostia: Ikastolen Elkartea, 1993. https://bdb.bertsozale.eus/web/liburutegia/view/3698-ahozkotasuna-i.-hezkuntzan.

Mendizabal, Mikel, and Kazabon, Antton. Bapaterako jarriak. Donostia: Ikastolen Elkartea, 1994.

Bibliography

Agirre, Antxoka. 2019. "Bertsolaritzaren historia: hedabideratzea, eragiletza eta proiektua (1823-2019). Ahots subalternoaren bizi-indarraren testigantza bat." Leioa: University of the Basque Country.

Aranburu, Antton; Iriondo, Joxe Mari. 1980. "Bertsolaritza gaur eta bihar." *Jakin*, 14-15 (apirila-iraila): 38-49.

Bolivar, Antonio. 2002. *Cómo mejorar los centros educativos*. Madrid: Editorial Síntesis SL.

Díaz Pimienta, Aléxix. 2014. *Método Pimienta para la Enseñanza de la Improvisación Poética (Oralitura).* Escripta Manent Ediciones.

Dorronsoro, Juanito. 2002. *Zumaiako bertso eskola: 20 urte kantari.* Zumaiako bertso eskola. ISBN: 84-607-6442-7

———. 1987. "Bertsolaritza Modernoaren Bideak." *Jakin*, 44 (uztaila-iraila): 7-33.

Eizagirre, Estitxu. 2007. "Bertso eskolak." *Bertso-eskolei buruzko lan ireki bat* (blog). (https://web.archive.org/web/20080516204720/http://www.argia.com/bertso-eskolak/argitalpenak). (Last retrieved: 18/01/2020 https://web.archive.org/web/20080516204720/http:/www.argia.com/bertso-eskolak/argitalpenak

Esnal, Pello. 1993. "Bat-bateko bertsogintzaren didaktika." *Jakin*, 75 (martxoa-apirila): 97-116.

Garzia, Joxerra. 1986. "Bertsolaritza in school curriculum." *Oral Tradition Journal*, Vol 22/2: 69-76. Bloomington: Slavica Publishers.

Garzia, Joxerra, Jon Sarasua, and Andoni Egaña. 2001. *The Art of Bertsolaritza: Improvised Basque Verse Singing.* Donostia: Bertsozale Elkartea.

Krichesky, Gabriela; Murillo Tordecilla, Javier. 2011. "Las comunidades profesionales de aprendizaje. Una estrategia de mejora para una nueva concepción de escuela." *Revista Iberoamericana sobre Calidad, Eficacia y Cambio en Educación.* Vol. 9/1.

Rodriguez, Fito. 1988. "Bertsolaritza, formarik gabeko heziketa." Donostia: University of the Basque Country.

Sarasua, Jon. 1993. "Herri mailako jarduna." *Jakin*, 75 (martxoa-apirila): 33-51.

———. 2014. "Transmisioaren garrantziaz." *Ahoa Bete Hots jardunaldiak.* Mintzola Ahozko Lantegia. (https://www.mintzola.eus/eu/files/ahozko-elkargunea/ahoa-bete-hotsartikuluak/2014-ahoa-bete-hots-transmisioaren-garrantziaz-jon-sarasua-1) (Last retrieved: 18/01/2020)

Zubiri, Harkaitz; Aierdi, Xabier; Retortillo, Alfredo. 2019. *Kultura ez da bat-batekoa. Bertsolaritza aztergai*. Bilbao: University of the Basque Country.

Zubiri, Harkaitz. 2016. "Kultur ekosistema sortzeko estrategia, bertsolaritza garaikidean transmisioa ulertzeko gako" ("Strategy for creating a cultural ecosystem, a key to understanding transmission in contemporary Bertsolaritza"). Europa bat-batean. International Improvised Singing Meeting. Academic Conferences. Donostia, July 2016.

Additional Sources

Bertsolaritzaren plaza digitala: https://bertsoa.eus/

Bertsozale Elkartea: https://www.bertsozale.eus/eu

Bertso eskolentzako webgunea: https://bertsoeskola.eus/

Hezkuntza arautuko formaziorako webgunea: https://bertsoikasgela.eus/

Mintzola Ahozko Lantegia: https://mintzola.eus/

Personal Interviews carried out by the author to the members of the Transmission Committee: Ane Labaka, Ixiar Eizagirre, Esti Alberdi, Mikel Artola, Josu Landeta, Oihane Perea, Asier Alcedo and Xan Alkhat (Between December 2019 and January 2020).

Xenpelar Dokumentazio Zentroa: http://bdb.bertsozale.eus/web/bertsoa/bilaketa

The Possible Impact and Benefits of a Self-Organized and Structured *Bertso-Eskola* on the Region and on the Bertso Community

Jone Uria Albizuri

Jone Uria Albizuri was born in Getxo in 1990. She studied mathematics at the University of the Basque Country (UPV/EHU), completing her master's degree at the Autonomous University of Madrid and her Ph.D at the University of the Basque Country (2017). She is currently an assistant professor at the Department of Mathematics of the School of Science and Technology of the University of the Basque Country. In addition, she is a bertsolari. She started performing at the improvisational poetry (Bertsolaritza) school of Algorta when she was twelve. Since then, she has participated in several championships, was a finalist in the Bizkaia championship for the last six competitions, and was a semifinalist in the Basque Country national championship for the last three years. She has performed in several bertso-saios (improvisational poetry gatherings) around the Basque Country. She is a member of the Bertsozale Elkartea (Association of Friends of Bertsolaritza) and the improvisational poetry school of Algorta.

Abstract

Celebrating its fortieth anniversary in 2020, the improvisational poetry school of Algorta is one of the oldest bertso-eskolak (bertso schools) in the Basque Country. It started as a meeting point for the bertsozales (lovers, fans of Basque improvisational poetry) in Algorta, as a place where people could sing bertsos and enjoy their shared passion for the craft. The Algorta school has now evolved into one of the most structured bertso-eskolas in the Basque Country, providing both a space in which children and young people begin their study of bertso technique and performance, and in which experienced adults can practice and improve their skills. In collaboration with other regional groups, the school plays an important role in the organization of bertso-saios (improvisational poetry gatherings) in Algorta and the Uribe Kosta region. In this paper, the author will explain how the Algortako Bertsolari Eskola (ALBE) is self-organized, will assess the impact of its work on the region and in the bertso community, and will identify some possible keys for success in a bertso-eskola.

The importance of bertso schools in the resurgence of bertsolaritza (practice of and movement around bertso) since the 1980s has been crucial. It is not possible to understand the current situation of bertsolaritza without the concept of the bertso-eskola. There are more than 150 bertso-eskolas in the whole Basque Country. Each one has its own structure, and there are very different kinds of them. Here we will focus our attention on one particular bertso-eskola because of its size and its ability to survive for many years in an environment, a priori, not ideal for bertsolaritza.

The aim of this article is to exhibit the current situation of one of the oldest bertso-eskolas in the Basque Country, Algortako Bertsolari Eskola (ALBE). Apart from being one of the oldest, it is an example of a well-structured bertso-eskola, playing a role not only as a bertso-eskola but also as a cultural organizer. We will use this example to question several issues regarding the role and definition of a bertso-eskola, both in the region and in the bertso community. Moreover, we will exhibit all the parts of this bertso-eskola, together with its different undertakings. We will try to explain why all the parts are important and crucial, and how they fit together within a single entity. We finally will focus our attention on the impact of such work and on the possible keys for ALBE's success.

The paper is organized as follows. First, we explain the geographical and sociological environment where ALBE was born and lives. In the historical review we also explain how ALBE is currently structured. Next, we try to offer a broader definition of a bertso-eskola. In the following two sections, we explain the role of ALBE as both a bertso-eskola in the traditional sense and as a cultural organizer. We later explain how these two projects complement each other. Finally, we show what the impact of ALBE is both at the regional level and in the community; and we conclude by giving some possible key elements which allow such a structure to work and survive for 40 years in a healthy and productive way.

Geographical, Socioeconomic, and Linguistic Environment

Algorta is a neighborhood in the town of Getxo, which is located on the west coast of Bizkaia (Biscay), a province of the Basque Autonomous Community. Getxo is part of the Greater Bilbao metro area and has about 77,000 inhabitants (Eustat, 2020). It is mostly residential and an economically wealthy area.

Inside Greater Bilbao, there is a subdivision called Uribe Kosta. Getxo is part of Uribe Kosta, and the other towns constituting this subdivision are: Barrika, Berango, Gorliz, Leioa, Lemoiz, Plentzia, Sopela, and Urduliz (Wikipedia, Uribe Kosta, 2019). Although according to Wikipedia, Erandio is not part of Uribe Kosta, for our purposes we will include it there, as ALBE works in collaboration with the town of Erandio for many purposes. Thus, when we talk about Uribe Kosta in this article, we will consider Erandio as part of it—in addition to the other towns mentioned.

According to Eustat, in Getxo the percentage of Basque speakers is 27% (Eustat, Getxo 2019), and in the rest of towns of Uribe Kosta the percentage is between 30 and 40%.

Brief History of Algortako Bertsolari Eskola

In Uribe Kosta, there already existed a tradition for bertso before the emergence of Algortako Bertsolari Eskola (ALBE). One could say that the emergence of ALBE helped to revive the interest in bertso in Uribe Kosta in the twentieth century. However, it is also known that in this region there were several bertsolaris (bertso improvisers). There is a precise and accurate history of bertsolaritza in Uribe Kosta during the period of 1900–1980 in (Paia Ruiz 2013). This was the period before the emergence of the ALBE bertso-eskola (Algortako Bertsolari Eskola, Alberen Historia Kronologikoki 2019).

Before the existence of ALBE, it is natural that no bertso-eskola existed in Uribe Kosta, as they were not yet "invented." The first bertso schools started to emerge in the 1980s, thanks in great part to Xabier Amuriza. Before that period, bertsolaritza was thought to be something you were born with. The skills needed to become a bertsolari were believed to be part of one's nature, as opposed to being possible to learn. However, Xabier Amuriza, who in 1980 won the Basque championship of bertsolaritza, started to claim that one could learn the art of singing bertsos. This idea that is nowadays accepted, was quite radical at the time. And it is one of the reasons why many bertso-eskolas were created in that period, at least in Bizkaia.

Just after winning the national contest on January 6, 1980, Xabier Amuriza gave a course in Bilbao, in which he spread his ideas mentioned above, among others. After that, some people started creating their own bertso-eskolas in their own towns. In this way, the first bertso-eskolas were created in Bizkaia, such as those in Santutxu (Bilbao), Mungia, and Algorta.

The people responsible for creating Algortako Bertsolari Eskola (ALBE) were Andoni Iriondo from Mendaro (Gipuzkoa), and Trino Azkoitia from Azpeitia (also in Gipuzkoa). At the time, they were implicated in Basque activism, which was rising significantly, and they were already convinced that they should do something to increase the impact of bertso in Algorta and surrounding areas. After receiving the course by Xabier Amuriza, they decided to create a bertso-eskola in Algorta, and that is how our bertso-eskola was born.

During the first two years, 1980–1982, the meeting place for the bertso-eskola was a room in Zabala public school in Algorta. At this stage, the bertso-eskolas consisted of informal meetings where people would sing old written bertsos and improvise as they were able. Later, bertso-eskolas began imparting more formal classes.

The period from 1983 to 1987 is called by some veterans of ALBE the golden era. The classes started to be more formal and many people from the euskaltegi (places where Basque language is taught) joined the bertso-eskola. ALBE was a place where people could interact just in Basque, and that was not common in Getxo at the time. At some point they even had more than 60 students, and they needed a second teacher to help them. The aim at that time was just to learn to sing bertsos in order to enjoy a good time in Basque with friends.

In 1988 there was a change of vision at the bertso-eskola. The rhythm of attendance was a bit lower again, and the organizers realized that at the heart of bertsolaritza was the figure of the bertsolari. They thought that Getxo and Uribe Kosta needed bertsolaris, and that the bertso-eskola should produce them. This idea also explains the name of the bertso-eskola—Algortako Bertsolari Eskola—which emphasizes the importance of the bertsolari. Motivated by these thoughts, Joseba Santxo, a member of ALBE, started to give bertsolaritza courses at the schools San Nikolas Ikastola (Algorta), Ander Deuna Ikastola (Sopela), and Gobela Ikastola (Leioa). Many children enrolled in those courses, and they rapidly extended to other schools too. From the efforts of this period came several people which have played a key role in the recent history of ALBE—such as bertsolaris, drivers and promoters of the bertso-eskola, some gai-jartzaile (the person who determines the topics about which the bertsolaris must improvise), and some judges. The aim at the time was that some of these children would join the bertso-eskola when older, and it worked as expected. However, between the years of 1990 and 1994, some members stopped going to the bertso-eskola and there was low attendance at the time.

With the goal of having more presence in the area, and to overcome the issue of losing people, in 1995 the bertso-eskola, with the name Algortako Bertsolari Eskola (ALBE), was officially registered and created as an association. It is then when they started to organize more public bertso activities, and the visibility and presence of bertsolaritza in Uribe Kosta rose significantly, bringing many new faces into ALBE. The principal purpose of organizing more activities and bertso-saios (improvisational poetry gatherings) was to generate a wider group of listeners and people fond of bertso, as this would provide a safer and richer ecosystem for the future young bertsolaris. In a few years, ALBE was organizing more than 20 performances in a year, in different towns and neighborhoods, of various styles, and throughout the whole year.

It is important to mention the relationships that started during this period were then, and continue to be, key for ALBE. In fact, ALBE received solid and generous treatment and deals with both the town hall and the kultur etxea (entity inside the town hall responsible for organizing cultural activities), which have since evolved into an agreement with the town hall and a collaborative work with the kultur etxea. Additionally, ALBE started to meet and work with other cultural associations in the region, and began organizing activities collaboratively around Getxo and other parts of Uribe Kosta. These collaborations are of relevance when understanding the way ALBE operates nowadays.

During the first years of the twenty-first century, the first bertso-eskolas at ALBE for solely young people were organized and offered. Until then, people of several ages, including teenagers, had been in the same group. These separate bertso-eskola classes for the youngest members were taught by adult members of ALBE. This was crucial, since in order to learn how to perform bertso and to improve, it is important to have a baseline and to train with people that are at a similar level and situation, at least when one is a beginner. For teenagers, it is important to have a safe environment that gives them the confidence to learn. During that period, some of the adults of the bertso-eskola took the responsibility of giving these lectures while some others assumed the work of organizing bertso activities and carrying out the accounting administration. It is important to mention that most of the responsibility for the latter fell into the hands of a single person.

Around 2005, the person mainly responsible for administration and the performances organized by ALBE, decided to leave his work in the hands of four other people of ALBE. This period was crucial, since for many associations that were born in the 80s and later, the inability to involve multiple generations in the management of the bertso-eskolas led to their disappearance. In ALBE's case, the four people decided to divide the responsibility among a broader group, which was later called the zuzendaritza (management committee). Since that period until now, the main body for decisions in ALBE is the zuzendaritza, which is formed by approximately 10 members of ALBE from different generations.

In 2009, by decision of the zuzendaritza, ALBE organized a joint strategic analysis about its current situation, problems of the time, and aims for the future. One of the decisions that was made during that analysis was that an employee was needed for the bertso-eskola. Until then, all the work had been done voluntarily. The dimensions of the bertso-eskola were increasing little by little, and some of the work that ALBE needed to do (staff and administrative issues, for instance) was incompatible with the schedules of the volunteers. After negotiating with the town hall and gaining some other public subsidies, ALBE managed to employ one person. ALBE became then the first bertso-eskola to have an employee, although nowadays there are more cases. Since then, ALBE has had four different employees in ten years. One of the fears when making that decision was whether the voluntarism of members would decrease as a result.

However, ten years later, one can say with certainty this has not been the case.

In 2019, ALBE organized another strategic analysis, taking advantage that the previous employee had left the job to ask ALBE members about the current situation of the organization, its current needs, and future aims. One of the conclusions was that most efforts of the zuzendaritza were directed at the organization of activities and the school for the teenagers, but that the adults' school was a bit abandoned and disorganized. Therefore, it was decided to distribute different areas of the bertso-eskola among different members within the zuzendaritza, as explained at the end of this section. Another important outcome were the agreed upon aims and role of ALBE as an organizer. Among them, that ALBE should give a place to our teenagers and youngest bertsolaris to perform, but also that the bertso-eskola should bring in a diverse spectrum of bertsolaris, in order to bring the peripheries into closer contact with ALBE. This must be understood in the context that, geographically speaking, Uribe Kosta is on the periphery of the Basque Country. Moreover, in the world of bertso, where everything is spoken in Basque, Algorta and Uribe Kosta are considered peripheral in that sense. Finally, ALBE also realized that they needed an employee who, apart from doing the administrative job, would be good at communication, social networks, and marketing. In recent years, this aspect has gained a lot of importance when organizing activities, so it was thought to be necessary.

Today ALBE is structured with a 10-person (give or take) zuzendaritza as its main body; teenager bertso-eskola groups; groups at primary schools in Uribe Kosta; an adult group; and an employee. The zuzendaritza, together with the employee, meets every month to decide the most important issues. As aforementioned, the responsibilities among the members of the zuzendaritza were distributed into roles such as: administrative duties, organization of activities, adults' bertso-eskola management, operation of teenagers' bertso-eskola, communication, and new ideas and development. Having described how zuzendaritza is structured, and before exploring the main parts of ALBE and seeing how they fit together, let us briefly discuss the definition of a bertso-eskola in general.

Definition of a Bertso-Eskola?

The most simple and obvious definition of a bertso-eskola is a place where people meet to perform bertsos. This broad definition could in principle, and does in practice, give rise to many different bertso-eskolas, from informal meetings among friends to well organized and structured official associations. In this sense, one could say that ALBE is one of the extreme cases of a highly organized and structured bertso-eskola, where offering a place for people to perform bertso is just one of its many aims. However, it is not the only bertso-eskola that works like that. In fact, many bertso-eskolas work as organizers of bertso activities in their towns.

The most general picture one could have of a bertso-eskola is probably the one that was described at the 2019 bertso-eguna in Barañain (Bertso eguna, bertsoa.eus, 2019). Bertso-eguna is a whole-day festival that has been organized by Bertsozale Elkartea for the last 50+ years. Until a few years ago, it was always celebrated in Donostia-San Sebastián (Gipuzkoa), but since 2018 it has been celebrated in different towns, such as Mungia (Bizkaia), Barañain (Navarre), and Aramaio (Araba). Moreover, the one in 2019 was the first bertso-eguna organized together with the entity in charge of driving the cohesion of bertso-eskolas all around the Basque Country, and that is why the topic of the bertso-saio in the afternoon was this one: "bertso-eskolas." One can be sure the bertsos sung were not just about meeting in a place to perform bertsos. There was also a topic about organizing a bertso-saio (Bertso eguna, bertsoa.eus, 2019). This did not happen by chance; all around the Basque Country, there are many bertso-eskolas that organize bertso-saios. According to the database of Xenpelar Dokumentazio Zentroa, 1,690 and 1,697 bertso activities were organized in 2018 and 2019, respectively, in the Basque Country. Among them, 1,445 and 1,443 were improvised bertso activities. The data about who organized each of the activities was only recorded for 912 and 809 of the total cases, respectively. If one calculates the percentage of activities that were organized by a bertso-eskola (among the activities with a known organizer), it is 20.83% in 2018 and 20.5% in 2019. It is important to mention that if one considers the total amount of bertso activities organized, these percentages go down to around 10 percent. Therefore, the real amount should be between these two percentages, but it is difficult to estimate, as one must make assumptions about the percentage of unknown organizers that could be a bertso-eskola. In any case, this data suggests that between one-tenth and one-fifth of improvised bertso activities are organized by the bertso-eskolas. Within these percentages, one can count more than fifty different bertso-eskolas participating as organizers. This reflects the job of the bertso-eskolas not only as informal places to improvise, or where the younger ones can learn to improvise, but also as organizing entities. This is a key point, as we shall see later in the case of ALBE, given that it leads to possible strategic choices and training of organizers which turns out to be of great importance and has been overlooked in years past to some extent.

Another function of a bertso-eskola should be to train not only bertsolaris but also judges and gai-jartzailes (topic setters). In some sense, the latter should happen automatically, since once a group of people is joined to perform bertso, someone would have to choose the topic to perform. However, in most bertso-eskolas this is done without much care, improvising the topics in the moment or looking at older topics used in contests and bertso-saios. A sign of that is the place it takes on the new website made for bertso-eskolas (Bertsoeskola Gaitegia, bertsoeskola.eus, 2019). In any case, the need to enforce the figure and the role of the gai-jartzaile is one of the concerns of the bertso community, as can be seen in the creation of the gai-jartzaile eskola promoted by Bertsozale Elkartea in 2015 with the aim of forming professional gai-jartzailes. The training of judges at bertso-eskolas is something that nowadays does not exist but could be an important future endeavor. We will see later how a bertso-eskola can provide the training for these two roles, in an informal and non-continued sense, in the case of ALBE. While this is not an ideal solution, it does allow for some minimal education in those roles.

ALBE as a Bertso-eskola

ALBE provides bertso classes for people of almost all ages. Since the very beginning of the history of ALBE, it was considered strategic to offer bertso classes at primary schools. In 2002, ALBE reached an agreement with the city council of Getxo to give classes at several schools. Later, with the project of Bertsozale Elkartea, many schools in Uribe Kosta have joined to offer bertso classes in their centers. Nowadays, such classes in Gorliz, Plentzia, Erandio, Leioa, Sopela, Urduliz, and Getxo are given by members of ALBE. In Getxo, it is still done by a particular formula agreed upon with the city council, but in the rest of the towns these classes are given thanks to a project called Bizkaiko Bertsozale Elkartea. However, it is important to emphasize that these classes are given by members of ALBE, which is a strategic choice both for ALBE and for the Bertsozale Elkartea. In fact, it is important to have referent people in the area as teachers, so that the children who are interested in bertso can inquire with them about possible activities or paths to follow outside of classes.

Apart from the classes for all students at each school, bertsolaritza is also offered in some schools as an extracurricular choice. Students that are interested in performing bertso can improve their skills there, before attending ALBE. Such classes are intended for students around 13–14 years, so that they continue on to ALBE once they reach around age 15. These kinds of classes are offered in Getxo, Leioa, and Sopela schools, and are given either by teachers from Bizkaiko Bertsozale Elkartea (also members of ALBE), or just members of ALBE. The decision to offer these courses was due to the growth of young students at

ALBE. At that time (around 2017), the people that were teaching classes to young people and children at ALBE were doing so completely voluntarily. This, together with the growth in number of students, made these classes untenable and not profitable. Hence, the decision to postpone the introduction into ALBE to later ages, and to offer extracurricular classes at schools—so that the children who eventually attend ALBE already have a good foundation and certain maturity. Moreover, it was agreed to begin symbolically asking for payment for such classes. It was symbolic in the sense that the price is very low, but it at least recognizes the effort and compromise of the lecturers; it emphasizes that the classes should be a place for fun, but also a place to learn; and it reminds both lecturers and students to take it with a bit of seriousness.

Regarding the classes that are offered at ALBE for youths, these started around the year 2000. Until then, all members of ALBE—youths and adults—had joint meetings. However, it was decided to offer lectures for youths separate from the adult ones. These classes are led by a teacher, usually a young member of ALBE. The generation born in or around the 1990s was the first one who received such lectures, and somehow, they understood that their role would be to offer them to younger ones. Nowadays, the students that grew up in ALBE at some point, are the ones who are giving classes to the new students. This tradition has somehow naturally worked, and it is important because it leads to strong relations among different generations. It also provides self-referentiality to the people in ALBE, and it does not create huge and long-term concerns, since one knows that the next generation will do the job at some point. Currently, there are three youth groups and three teachers.

Once people reach adulthood (meaning 18 years old), they pass to ALBE's adult bertso-eskola. This step is not always easy, as in the adult bertso-eskola there are a lot of people, of different ages, interests, ambitions, and levels. In the last reflection period, this was one of the hottest points. It is not easy to provide a common place for a large amount of people with different interests and skills, where they can all achieve their goals. To handle this issue, three members from the zuzendaritza committee took on the responsibility of analyzing the situation and offering a possible solution. They asked to each of the ALBE members about their availability, goals, and interests, and the organization suggested a possible way to solve the problems that were being found. Nowadays, the big group that used to meet on Tuesdays is split into several smaller and mixed groups, and a new group on Wednesdays has been formed for people who aspire to compete in contests, perform at town halls, and improve their skills more seriously than just for fun. Most of the members in that second group are young improvisers. On the other hand, it was decided to organize an informal meeting point in a cultural center called Azebarri with all the people from the bertso-eskola. This happens one Thursday every month. Although members of ALBE have varied interests and take classes in split groups and on different days, all are still members of the same bertso-eskola, and these days give the opportunity to have fun all together and share thoughts with one another. All these efforts have allowed the performance of the bertso-eskola to be fluid and fruitful in a way it had not been in prior years. The role of the zuzendaritza and of its members, who took the responsibility to handle this particular situation, has been very important to the smooth functioning of the bertso-eskola. Had it not been for the zuzendaritza's intervention, the youngest and most ambitious improvisers might have either quit or taken their talent elsewhere.

ALBE as a Cultural Organizer

As mentioned in the section about the brief history of ALBE, in 1995, together with officially creating the association ALBE, it was decided to start organizing more bertso activities in order to gain presence in town and the surrounding areas. A few years later, ALBE was already organizing more than 20 activities per year, and nowadays it organizes more than 30 every year. The importance of organizing this amount of bertso-saios resides not only in the number, but more importantly in the type of each activity and the purposes each satisfies, the distribution of activities throughout all Uribe Kosta and throughout the year, the joint work with other organizers, and the resulting possibility of bringing different bertsolaris and giving opportunities to the local ones. We will examine these key points in a deeper way one by one, but before doing so, we list here the main activities organized by ALBE, with a brief description of the nature of each.

ABRA SARIKETA: This contest for young improvisers (18–24 years of age) is celebrated every year, around February. It lasts one day and has a dinner format, in which six bertsolaris take part. There is always one bertsolari from each province, constituting five of the participants (Lapurdi, Lower Navarre, and Zuberoa are considered a single entity for this contest); the sixth bertsolari is always a member of ALBE. The jury is usually formed by three judges from three different provinces who act as judges in official contests.

KANPOMARTXO: Celebrated every year around the end of March or in April, it is a day organized jointly with Berbots, an association working on the promotion of Basque in Erandio. The presence of bertso, usually at midday, is highlighted by the performance of two improvisers singing freely, without topics.

ESKUALDEKO TXAPELKETA: Celebrated every two years, the first edition was held in 2016, after the restructuring of the official contest of Bizkaia. It is an informal contest for improvisers of Uribe Kosta. In the past two editions, there were 24 improvisers, a team of 7–8 gai-jartzailes, and 7–8 judges. It is usually held in three days: two afternoons for qualifying rounds and a whole day for semifinals and the final. The performances take place in bars and informal contexts.

UDABERRIKO BERTSO AFARIA: It takes place every two years and is a bertso dinner where two improvisers take part. It is celebrated in Getxo, in different restaurants in each edition.

BALKOITIK BALKOIRA: It takes place every year, around the end of June. It is celebrated in the old port of Algorta, where two bertsolaris improvise on two balconies. This kind of bertso-saio comes from old traditions. It is one of the most popular activities we organize, and it attracts people who are not usual bertsozales.

LEIOAKO JAIETAKO SAIOA: This event happens every year, during the festivals of Leioa, which take place around San Juan's Day (June 24). It is what it is known as a bertso-jaialdi (a bertso-saio that is held on a stage with a gai-jartzaile). In this case, there are four improvisers. This format is repeated in most bertso-saios held during festivals. It is jointly organized with Leioa's town hall and festivals committee.

SOPELAKO JAIETAKO SAIOA: The same kind of activity as in Leioa, but around San Pedro's Day (June 28), it is jointly organized with Sopela's town hall and festivals committee.

BERTSO JAIALDI MUNDIALA: This event takes place every year, in the second week of July. It is the biggest bertso festival we organize in terms of audience size (700–800 people). Until the year 2019, it was held on a stage under a big tent, but since a big theater called Muxikebarri was inaugurated in Algorta, this festival is now celebrated there. It is always a thematic bertso-jaialdi, where the topics are prepared carefully and in advance by a large team. This festival also attracts people not typically found at other bertso activities.

GORLIZKO JAIETAKO SAIOA: The same as in Leioa, but around Santiago's Day (July 25), this event is jointly organized with the town hall of Gorliz.

ALGORTAKO JAIETAKO SAIOAK: During the festivals of Algorta, around San Inazio's Day (July 31), we organize one bertso-jaialdi (as in Leioa and the other town festivals) per day. In total, three to four bertso-saios are jointly organized with the festivals committee of Algorta.

BERTSO MARATOIA: On July 31, as part of the festivals of Algorta, after celebrating the festival in a town hall at midday, we continue with a bertso-bazkari (a bertso-saio held after lunch) and long bertso-poteo (a bertso-saio where bertsolaris improvise from bar to bar), where two of the four improvisers of the midday festival continue singing after lunch and in bars during the whole day until late at night. This is also one of the most popular bertso activities—not necessarily with regards to the audience size, but definitely in regard to quality.

ERROMOKO JAIETAKO SAIOAK: During the festivals of Erromo (a neighborhood of Getxo), two bertso activities are celebrated every year around the first week of August. One is a bertso-jaialdi with four improvisers and the gai-jartzaile, and the other one is a bertso-poteo. It is jointly organized with the festivals committee of Erromo.

PORTU ZAHARREKO JAIETAKO BERTSO SAIOAK: During the festivals of the old port of Algorta, which are held around mid-August, we organize two bertso activities. One consists of two bertsolaris performing freely in the evening, and the other one takes place just before the awards ceremony of a gastronomic competition. The first one is a new bertso activity launched by us, and the second one has more tradition. The event is jointly organized with the committee of festivals of Portu Zaharra.

ERANDIOKO JAIETAKO BERTSO SAIOA: In the festivals of Erandio, which are held at the end of August, we organize a bertso festival similar to those of Leioa, Sopela, etc., with four improvisers and the gai-jartzaile. It is jointly organized with Berbots.

HITZAREN DANTZA: Celebrated in September, we mix traditional Basque dances with bertso. Different dance associations from Uribe Kosta take part, dancing seven dances—the typical dances of each province of the Basque Country—in each square. Subsequently, three bertsolaris perform freely in each square. We celebrate a public luncheon in the town hall and bertsolaris also sing after lunch.

BERTSO AFARI TEMATIKOA: This is celebrated every two years, previously in the spring and now in autumn. It is a bertso-afari (same as a bertso-bazkari, but after dinner) where there is a theme, such as western, mafia, or Irish, which dictates how the general ambient will be. The improvisers are given topics related to this overarching theme.

BIHOTZA GAZTE: It is celebrated every two years, also in autumn. It is a bertso-saio where elderly, seasoned bertsolaris perform. The name Bihotza Gazte refers to this fact, as it means "young heart." We try to bring bertsolaris who performed for a long time but nowadays are not that active.

SOPELAKO BERTSO JIRA: This is celebrated at the beginning of December and is in the format of a bertso-poteo. It is jointly organized with the municipal association of Uribe Kosta (Uribe Kostako mankomunitatea).

ERANDIOKO BERTSO JIRA: It is celebrated toward the end of December, and it is also a bertso-poteo like the one in Sopela. It is jointly organized with Berbots.

ALBE GALA: Celebrated at the end of December, it also coincides every two years with the awards ceremony of a written bertso contest that we organize. Every two years, it also coincides with an award we give to a bertsolari for her or his trajectory. It is a festival we organize to remember all the activities we have had during the year and to have fun all together.

GAZTEEN SAIOAK: During the whole year, we also organize bertso-saios where our youngest improvisers can perform in public. Such occasions are usually in small neighborhood festivals, such as the day when Olentzero comes (December 24) or San Juan's Day.

Naturally, the organization of all these activities takes work, time, and money. Regarding economic issues, it has to be mentioned that ALBE has had (and continues to have) a good relationship with the town hall of Getxo, which provides the funds needed to organize most of the activities that are organized in Getxo. The rest of the activities are usually funded by the local government of each place, or by the Association of Municipalities of Uribe Kosta. Regarding the efforts and time it requires, deciding which bertsolaris will be invited to act in each event, choosing the theme and topic (for some of them), and hosting the improvisers and co-organizers the whole day of the event, are just some of the things to consider. The hard work pays off, however, benefiting individuals, communities, and ALBE itself.

How the two projects complement each other

One might think that ALBE as a bertso-eskola and as a cultural organizer are two independent structures with different aims within the same association. However, that would be a false assumption, and this section will demonstrate why.

At the beginning (as mentioned in the historical section about ALBE), the principal reason to increase the number of activities was to improve the impact on the region and consequently attract more people to the bertso-eskola. While it is not currently one of the most important aims, it still plays that role. People need references, and the bertso-saios organized by ALBE provide that. If one has seen improvisers performing in the squares of his or her hometown since childhood, and if one has seen people enjoying and having fun with bertso, it is more likely he or she will become interested in it. For the children who study at school what bertsos are in theory, it helps them to understand what bertsolaritza is by seeing it live, in practice. This is true not only for the youngest ones but also for adults. Many of the people who are part of the bertso-eskola learned about ALBE through the activities organized by them. It is important because it gives referentiality to bertso, and also to ALBE as a local and regional entity.

Another important role of organizing cultural events is that it gives local improvisers the opportunity to perform. It can be difficult to make the jump from the bertso-eskola to performing at squares or in theaters. Many people leave bertso at this stage, either because of a bad experience, loss of self-confidence, or just because, in many senses, it is a hard transition. In that aspect, the bertso-eskola can offer beginners a safe and comfortable place to start. The number of activities organized by ALBE gives an opportunity to many young improvisers in the bertso-eskola. If ALBE were not the organizer of such activities, it is possible that each organizer would choose its two to four favorite improvisers, thus reducing the opportunities for local young people. ALBE, with its knowledge of each place that organizes activities, can choose appropriate improvisers for each. ALBE can even provide the exciting opportunity to those young improvisers to sing with the people they admire and respect, which is important in strengthening their passion for bertso.

As mentioned before, the bertso-eskolas are not currently structured to learn how to become a gai-jartzaile. And yet, the formation of gai-jartzailes is a concern of the bertso community. It has been a difficult task, however, and in most cases the gai-jartzaile is someone from the town or from the organizing association that is not necessarily close to the bertso world. In the case of ALBE, some of the activities it organizes—such as Abra Sariketa, Bertso Jaialdi Mundiala, Uribe Kostako Txapelketa, or Bertso Afari Tematikoa—are activities where the topics are decided and discussed in small groups. These groups are usually formed by people from ALBE, both improvisers and non-improvisers. In those groups, one learns what it is to organize a bertso-saio, how to structure the different activities, how to order the themes, and how to present them. This provides a way of seeing who might be interested in this kind of role, so that, for instance, for festival performances ALBE can ask these people to be the gai-jartzaile. In those cases, they do the job on their own, which leads to the formation of experienced (even if not professional) gai-jartzailes. This is really important, for it is difficult nowadays to create a circuit around the whole Basque Country for gai-jartzailes similar to that of bertsolaris. Usually the gai-jartzaile is a local person, which may be an important factor to do the job well. Even local gai-jartzailes, however, need to be valued and important figures. ALBE, in that sense, through its activities, helps its members gain experience and ensures quality at the performances at the same time.

Another important role in the bertso community (also of big concern) is that of an organizer. It is not a trivial task to organize a bertso-saio. There are many things to take into account. For instance, the technical part is crucial in such an event: both the audience and the bertsolaris need to hear themselves in an appropriate manner. When bertsolaris arrive to a town, they need someone to attend to them, to inform them about anything if needed, and so on. The bertsolari needs to feel that he or she is taken into account and is somehow part of the town at the moment; otherwise, the performance could be unsatisfactory for both the audience and the improvisers. Many organizers are either not aware of, or ignore, some of these aspects, and it is important to have references in order to learn them. In ALBE, as there are many years of experience in organizing activities, one can both learn from the previous ones and try to teach the next generations that bertsolaris must always feel comfortable when they go to a town, and how one should act in order to achieve this.

Finally, bertso-saios also play a social role for the people that form the bertso-eskola. All kind of members of ALBE—some who work, some who haven't attended in years and go to listen, some who left to perform years ago, some who were a crucial part of ALBE at some point—unite during these activities and have fun together. While one can forget this aspect of such activities, it is probably one of the most important.

The Impact on the Region and the Ecosystem of Bertso

To understand the possible impact of ALBE on the region, one could look at the data obtained in the last two years about bertso activity in the region. Even though ALBE organizes many activities, those only constitute about 50% of the improvised bertso-saios organized in Uribe Kosta per year (according to the Xenpelar Dokumentazio Zentroa database). This indicates that there is a huge offering of bertso activities in the region. Comparing, in area, Uribe Kosta with the whole Basque Country, and taking into account the number of performances organized in the Basque Country per year, in Uribe Kosta there should be 6 yearly activities, whereas there are actually around 60. However, it is true that the population in Uribe Kosta is quite high when compared with the population density of the Basque Country as a whole. Taking into account the population, there should be around 70 activities in Uribe Kosta in comparison to the whole Basque Country. This means that in that sense, we are slightly below but close to the average. For a region where the percentage of Basque speakers is around 30%, these are significant numbers. Moreover, the fact that there are several local and independent organizers, apart from ALBE, is also significant, as it means the region itself has passion for and interest in bertso. It would not be an exaggeration to say that the existence and work of ALBE has been a driver of this situation.

Additionally, it helps that ALBE is familiar with other entities and active people in the region. The relationships ALBE has with various festival committees, Basque promoters, and institutional entities (due, in part, to organizing many activities jointly with other organizations) strengthens the bertso ecosystem. Not only that, but it allows coordination of schedules, so that there are no two bertso-saios at the same time in two neighboring areas. We can also ensure that different bertsolaris will visit our region during the year, so that we can offer the audience a more diverse window of bertsolaritza than if each activity were independently organized. This would not be possible without a significant number of activities, as the range of bertsolaris one can bring during a year varies. As mentioned before, it is likely that independent organizers might repeat improvisers who are trendier at a given moment. One of the aims of ALBE is to give an opportunity to improvisers with different backgrounds, origins, genders, and ages. This way, one can create a wider culture and knowledge of bertsolaritza in the region, which is of great importance.

Apart from on Uribe Kosta, the work of ALBE has an impact on the whole community of bertso. According to the data from Xenpelar Dokumentazio Zentroa, in 2018 and 2019 ALBE was the organizer of approximately 2% of the improvised bertso activities in the Basque Country. Considering that a total of 50 bertso-eskolas are responsible for between 10 and 20 percent of all bertso activities, this is a huge amount for a single bertso-eskola and needs to be taken into account.

Keys for Success: Compromise, Passion, Organization, Cohesion, and Fun

ALBE's history and current reality exists neither by chance nor without cost. Behind it all is a lot of people's work, contributions, and efforts—most of them voluntary. It is not easy to completely understand how and why this has worked, and still works so well, but in what follows we attempt to identify some of the possible keys for this success.

Throughout the past 40 years, the commitment of many people has led to these positive results. While it is important to ensure there will be people who are committed to ALBE in this way, each of the members must to be able to choose their personal level of commitment. This is not always an easy thing. First of all, one cannot ask for a commitment without offering anything in return. Naturally, then, if so many people have been (and today are) committed to ALBE, it is because they get something back. It is important to not forget this fact and to highlight it. A bertso-eskola needs people that will not leave it just as soon as they come. It needs people to give bertso lectures to the youngest, people to organize events, people to make decisions . . . These things are not doable without committed members.

As mentioned, all this work and commitment is unthinkable in the absence of passion. All the members of ALBE have something in common, and it is their passion for bertso. In such a sociolinguistic environment, this passion interlaces people together in a strong way. Each member has *f* own way of exercising this passion, but ultimately it is the same feeling that unites them.

Part of the success of ALBE has also been in guessing how to self-organize. In each period of its existence, it has adopted different structures and ways of organization, without fearing change—and most of the time it has found the right solution for each hurdle. To make the appropriate guess each time, it is key to have different opinions, to listen to each other, and to take into account as many voices as possible; and then to decide according to that. This is not always something easy to do, but it is key to survive as an entity.

Another important factor that has been crucial in ALBE is cohesion. As is said in the coda of one of the bertsos describing ALBE, "There are many voices, but a unique heart."

Lau letratxo elkarren ondoan...
akronimoa da, brabo!
Eta atzean bertso-eskola bat...
parkatu, askoz gehiago!
A, L, B eta ondoan E,
ALBE lez ezagunago,
bertsozale bik sortu zutena
gaur baino askoz lehenago.
Laurogeian sortu zuten eta
ez ote dugu arraro
hainbeste urtez iraun izana
bertsogintzaren abaro.
Sekretutxo bat badauka, baina,
irauteak aroz aro:
ALBEn ahotsak ugari daude,
bihotza bakarra dago!

It is difficult to maintain cohesion in such a large group of people with different ages, goals, commitment levels, and interests. Moreover, within a structured entity, it is typical to have smaller groups of people which are more cohesive. However, it is crucial to maintain unity within the whole group as well, and many of ALBE's activities have this aim.

Last but not least, ALBE is a place where all the members have fun together. This is probably one of the reasons why bertso-eskolas blossomed so rapidly and why they are still alive. ALBE is a place where people have fun together by improvising, learning from each other, organizing activities, and improving their skills. It seems obvious, but sometimes one might forget this aspect, as simple as it is crucial. Without fun, ALBE would likely not have survived and thrived for 40 years.

References

Algortako Bertsolari Eskola (ALBE), Alberen Historia Kronologikoki (2019). http://www.albe.eus/alberen-historia-kronologikoki

Bertso eskolak, Bertso eguna (2019). https://bertsoa.eus/saioak/2019-01-26-baranain-42064

Bertso eskolak antolatzaile, Bertso eguna (2018). https://bertsoa.eus/bertsoak/16174-bertso-saioa-antolatzeko-lan-banaketa

Bertsoeskola, Gaitegia (2019). https://bertsoeskola.eus/gaitegia/

Bertsozale Elkartea, Gai-jartzaile eskola (2014). https://www.bertsozale.eus/eu/albisteak/gai-jartzaile-eskola-abiatuko-da-urrian

Bertsozale Elkartea, Bertsolaritzaren mapa (2019). https://bdb.bertsozale.eus/web/mapa/bertso-eskolak

Eustat, Getxoko datu estatistikoak. http://eu.eustat.eus/municipal/datos_estadisticos/getxo.html

Paia Ruiz, Fredi (2013), "Uribe Kostako Bertsolaritza", in *Getxoko Kultur Etxea*, Labayru ikastegia.

Wikipedia, Uribe Kosta (2019). https://en.wikipedia.org/wiki/Uribe-Kosta

Wikipedia, Getxo (2019). https://en.wikipedia.org/wiki/Getxo

Xenpelar Dokumentazio Zentroa

Beyond Linguistic Practices: Verse Schools as Prime Locus for the Co-construction of Youth Identity and Linguistic Identity

Miren Artetxe Sarasola

Miren Artetxe is a bertsolari and currently a lecturer in the School of Education, Philosophy and Anthropology at the University of the Basque Country. After receiving a BA in Basque linguistics at the University of the Basque Country, she completed a master's degree in cognitive science and language at the University of Barcelona in Catalonia. In 2019, she finished her Ph.D dissertation on the sociology of language and linguistic anthropology. Her current areas of interest are language practices among young people, the processes of legitimization of new speakers, the construction of youth identities, and the influence of gender systems and feminist practices, all within the cultural and social framework of bertsolaritza.

Abstract

When investigating the linguistic habits of young people, non-linguistic practices and identities are seldom taken into account. The idea that arises in this work is that the linguistic identity of young people, and therefore their linguistic practices, are closely related to youth identity. In this research, which was carried out in the bertso-eskola of Bernart Etxepare High School in Baiona (Northern Basque Country), we analyze the relationship between the linguistic behaviors of the young people and the construction of their youth identities. Indeed, in a sociolinguistic environment in which being competent in Basque is a marked characteristic among young people, the participants of the bertso schools have the habit of using Basque not only in the bertso schools, but also among their friends. By analyzing the bertso schools as a community of practice, it has been possible to analyze, at the same time, the relationship between group characteristics and individual identities, and the relationship of non-linguistic practices with linguistic practices. From the interviews carried out with 14 young people and the ethnographic work, some significant characteristics of the community of practice are pointed out, and it is argued that through these characteristics the members of the bertso schools develop a way of being young in Basque.

Introduction

In the sociolinguistic context of the Northern Basque Country (hereinafter NBC), living in Basque and being young are highly singular factors. And young people relating to each other using mainly Basque language is even more uncommon. In fact, the youth culture in the NBC is mainly consumed in French (Baxok et al. 2007, 89). Young people have access to all kinds of French (or English, or Spanish) podcasts, music, films, YouTube channels, television series, books, and magazines. In a society where the French language is seen as modern and fit for all purposes, Basque is not seen to be very "cool."[1]

So, knowledge of Basque among young people in the NBC is the characteristic of a minority, and the habit and desire to speak Basque among friends is even more singular. One way to positively embody a singular identity is to have a positive interpretation of that identity—in other words, identifying oneself with a style, not only with speaking Basque, but also with a way of being young and Basque-speaking. And that cannot be achieved by oneself.

This is one of the reasons why Bernart Etxepare High School is a good case study[2] for young people at a bertso school.

1 This is evident in research carried out on the opinion of non-Basque speakers about Spanish: "Because Basque is not cool or modern compared with Spanish" (Amorrortu, Ortega, Idiazabal, and Barreña 2009, 109). The same may be considered to be true in the NBC with regard to French.

2 Bernart Etxepare High School is the only high school in the Seaska Ikastola network, the Basque language immersive schooling network. It is in Baiona, where all primary, secondary, and final level immersion model NBC students come together. (In the education system of the Southern Basque Country, it would

In fact, young people who are members of the bertso school make intensive use of Basque. In addition to at bertso school, they mainly use Basque in their relationships with friends outside that context. In this work, based on interviews and ethnographic work with young people in the bertso school, I have analyzed the bertso school as a community of practice in order to understand how the Basque language is intertwined with young people's identities, and to emphasize the importance of this close relationship.

As young people meet weekly at bertso school, in addition to practicing bertsos they also have conversations and develop relationships and ways of doing things together (Eckert and McConnell-Ginet, 1992: 97). They share values and ideas. They create a group identity. And there are some communities of practice characteristics that may be useful for bertso school members to develop their youth identity: for instance, an atmosphere of group trust; experience in speaking and overcoming embarrassment; a tendency to reflect; and activism.

Since bertsolaritza is a Basque language practice, these conversations, these relationships, these ways of doing things, are all created in Basque, and they develop linguistic identity interactively with other elements of identity. In other words, they intertwine linguistic identity with youth identity, creating a particular way of being young and Basque speaking.

Background and Theoretical-Analytical Framework

Communities of Practice

Penelope Eckert and Sally McConnell-Ginet used the concept of communities of practice to theorize the co-construction of language and gender identities in the 1990s (Eckert and McConnell-Ginet 1992a, 1992b, 1995). The community of practice was defined as follows:

---

be the equivalent of the fourth (last) year of Compulsory Secondary Education and the two additional, final years of secondary education).

> A community of practice is an aggregate of people who come together around mutual engagement in some common endeavour. Ways of doing things, ways of talking, beliefs, values, power relations in short practices emerge in the course of this mutual endeavour. A community of practice is different as a social construct from the traditional notion of community, primarily because it is defined simultaneously by its membership and by the practice in which that membership engages. Indeed, it is the practices of the community and members' differentiated participation in them that structures the community socially. (Eckert and McConnell-Ginet 1992b, 97)

A community of practice is not, therefore, defined by a social category, a language variant, a place, or a particular population. A community of practice, as the name implies, is defined by the practices carried out by that community.

Each person's environment is made up of different communities of practice. We build ourselves in the communities in which we participate as individuals, defining our identity through the processes of creation and development of those communities. And in these communities of practice, each speaker "becomes an actor and an agent, reflecting on the type of connection she/he makes with the language and the characteristics of those communities" (Hernández 2005: 51).

From a holistic point of view, rather than analysing linguistic identities and practices in isolation, the communities of practice concept allows us to analyse identity in its complexity as a network linked to other sociocultural elements. The explanatory force of the community of practice theory relays, among other factors, on examining the link between language practices and other social practices. This approach allows us to not only relate certain linguistic forms to certain social practices, but also to understand how social meanings are embodied in language (Eckert 2006: 685).

Youth Identities

Analysis of bertso school practice as a community allows us to observe two interactions: on one hand, the mutual influence which exists between personal subjectivity and group identities, and on the other, the co-construction of linguistic identity and other identities (for instance, youth identity).

Youth identity is closely linked to youth cultures. One can identify oneself as a young person—and others will identify one as such—if one can find traits that belong to a youth culture in one's habits: a certain attire, a particular use of social media, a certain musical taste, a certain style, among other factors. I will use a definition by Carles Feixa to delineate the concept of youth culture:

> In a broad sense, youth cultures refer to the way in which young people's social experiences are expressed collectively through the construction of distinctive lifestyles, set mainly in their free time, or in interstitial positions of the institutional sphere. In a more restricted sense, they define the emergence of "youth micro-societies," with significant degrees of autonomy with respect to "adult institutions" (Feixa 1998).

Feixa speaks in the plural and avoids discussing youth cultures in the singular, emphasizing the diversity and heterogeneity of youth cultures. In fact, youth cultures are diverse, constantly changing, have blurred boundaries, and interact with one another. They may be more aesthetically marked, more visible, or seemingly imperceptible, but they all have a specific style that includes both material and immaterial elements (Feixa 1998: 201).

A young person does not have to have the same style throughout her or his youth, and she or he can take from one culture and then from another, creating her or his own style and building different levels of identification with different youth cultures. This will, of course, be influenced by the communities of practice in which the young person takes part—especially communities of practice made up of young people.

Young people's styles, enthusiasm, beliefs, thoughts, and value systems—even feelings of love, anger, or injustice—are often underestimated by adults. Unlike gender, class and other social conditions, youth cannot be maintained over time, so why worry about it?.

Moreover, young people—even upper-class young people, young men, and those who hold other social privileges—have a very modest capacity for decision-making and control over the conditions that structure their lives. Adult decision-making institutions generally regulate their decision-making options. Precisely because they have limited resources to control their lives, some groups of young people gain enough skills to self-affirm, create, and recreate a culture of their own. Language is a tool which expresses that style while constructing it.

Methodology

Interviews with young people at the bertso school, and the field work carried out there, is the basis for this research. Focusing on the meaning of being a member of the bertso school community for young people, and paying attention to the connection of bertso school membership to youth identity and Basque language practices, I carried out 14 semi-structured interviews with members of the Bernart Etxepare High School bertso school.[3]

Observation was my primary research tool. In addition to discourses about young people's experiences, I observed bertsolaritza and bertso school social practices, bertsolaritza summer camps, bertso schoolteachers, listeners of bertsolaritza, session organizers, bertsolaris and bertsolaritza members, and social practices carried out by members of the school community of practice.

3 Of the fourteen young people, eight socialized as girls, and six as boys. From the 2013–2014 academic year to the 2018–2019 academic year, girls and boys who had taken part in the bertso school for two or three consecutive years were interviewed, and all those interviewed were between the ages of 15 and 18.

I would also like to mention the importance of informal conversations. When carrying out participatory observation, it is not advisable to turn interviews held in the context of this fieldwork into surveys (Jociles 2016). However, semi-structured conversations that take place in a formal context are not the only conversations which serve as sources of data. Furthermore, there is a continuum between interviews designed specifically for research, and informal conversations held during fieldwork. There were many informal conversations which took place during this research, and which were of paramount importance in orienting it. These conversations sometimes helped me to better understand ideas which had emerged in formal conversations, and on other occasions they enabled me to see objects of study which had not been visible in the formal conversations.

Data Presentation and Analysis

Bernart Etxepare Bertso School. In Basque, Both in Verse and in Prose

At the Bernart Etxepare bertso school, the aim is to practice bertsolaritza and to train oneself in bertsos. When interviewees are asked about bertso school activities, however, what comes up most often in conversation is not bertsolaritza. It is well known that bertso school is a place for bertsos, but when they mention the activities related to bertso school that are most meaningful to them, the ones that stand out are non-bertso-centered.

In fact, bertso school dynamics create situations for relaxation and conversation. Not only is it permissible at bertso school, but it is also necessary for there to be dialogue between the members of the group, for them to joke with one another, to talk between one exercise and the next, to discuss both members' bertso topics, and to have long, in-depth discussions.

> Igor: Also, the atmosphere among us was already really good, yeah, really good, for the three years of high school. And we used to go to the bertso workshop, in principle, to make bertsos, but we've spent who knows

> how many hours laughing out loud, telling each other stuff, talking about this, talking about that, eating together... So yeah, you go to the bertso workshop to make bertsos, in principle, but it doesn't stop there; there are a thousand other things we've done that aren't bertsos.

On the other hand, extracurricular activities that the bertso school organizes outside the school are mentioned by the young people. Significantly, as many (or more) of these activities are organized by the students themselves as by the bertso school. Listening to bertso sessions, meetings with other bertso schools, experiences at bertso summer camps, and bertso parties, are among the activities the young people enjoy. In those contexts, the importance of speaking and conversations comes up:

> Allande: I don't know if these relationships can only be developed during normal bertso school activities or not... Yes, we have been working on those relationships all the time we have spent outside of bertso school, and so on... Yes, we have had bertso sessions and parties and so on... a lot. We go out together a lot, but sometimes we get together at a house and spend the whole night talking and stuff like that [. . .] I think speaking and so on is very important.

When students talk about the bertso school world, the nature of their group, the way they feel in their group, and their development within the group, there are some ways of talking, ways of doing things, and values that consistently emerge.

> Nekane: But what is unique about bertso school is that the same thing brings us together. Bertsolaritza brings us together, with all its values, and so in the end it's a sort of way of life. You learn a lot of things from the relationships. We're not the same, but we do have some of the same values about some things.

According to Eckert, members of communities of practice position themselves as a group in relation to the outside world:

> This includes the common interpretation of other communities, and of their own practice with respect to those communities, and ultimately with the development of a style - including a linguistic style - that embodies these interpretations. (Eckert 2006, 683–684)

In fact, the relationship with the Basque language and the use of the Basque language are, among other things, the factors which define the members of the bertso school community of practice's style.

> Interviewer: What changes from a 'normal' atmosphere to a bertso school atmosphere?
>
> Uhaina: Everything. For starters, the Basque language, okay... Yes. Most of us, all of us who go to bertso school, most of us speak Basque most of the time. I think so. And... everything, well... everything is different... well... there are two different worlds in one world.

Situation of Confidence

Creating an atmosphere of trust and empathy for practicing bertsolaritza is a necessary condition for bertso training—and for a bertso school to thrive. Improvisation always brings with it fear and attraction towards the abyss it creates. With improvisation, among other things, the person performing comes up against her or his own limitations: with the inability to say what she or he wants to say. With the frustration of thinking one thing and saying another. With being stuck in the middle of a bertso, unable to move forward. With saying something that makes no sense, in order to end a bertso. And to assume this publicly and optimistically (even if the audience is small and its members are known)—indeed if the process of bertso creation is to be a source of enjoyment—then an atmosphere of trust is essential.

An empathic bond between members is the main essential condition for creating a good atmosphere for bertso, but it is more than just an essential condition. The empathy between the members is formed by making and performing bertsos. When a member is not singing, she or he is observing what somebody else is singing. She or he can tell when that schoolmate is at ease and when she or he is having a hard time, for example. When things become impossible, members develop strategies to manage with that uncomfortable situation. "I have nothing," says one of the bertsolaris, meaning that she needs time. "Well, it's shit, but I'll say it anyway," she might warn otherwise, apologizing to the audience as much as she is asking the audience to be forgiving. It is a contract. And all the listeners try to make the job easier for someone who is struggling. They do this through gestures, through silence, through explicit support (saying part of the rhyme out loud, but softly, so that she or he can go on if stuck, for example), and, above all, by not being judgemental. Neither how the bertso gets completed, nor what is said in it, is judged. It is the trust, acceptance, and good-naturedness among the bertsolaris that is paramount.

> Jokin: Okay, so, for instance... all of us get out there to sing, and that makes it... it creates a sort of safety between all of us, and voilà we see some people screwing up, we see others throwing some good bertsos, different stuff, and I don't know... I think that is above all what creates some security, we're singing... we're ready to throw anything, a shitty bertso or a good one or whatever, in front of them and we all know, it's nothing, it doesn't matter, we can throw whatever we want..

Taking the Floor, Shedding One's Embarrassment, Taking the Floor

Conscious of one's vulnerability, and with some protection from the group, making bertsos becomes an act of self-affirmation. Taking a breath in front of others, breathing out with one's voice, singing and speaking, one's body in front of others, making one's discourse audible to everyone.

Speaking in itself implies agency (Duranti 2004), and taking the floor in bertsolaritza is also affirming oneself: this is my voice; I am here; this is me. At bertso school, it is a process of shedding one's embarrassment to take the floor. As one builds up trust with the team, embarrassment's ability to paralyze weakens. And the progress is noticeable. One becomes comfortable in one's own skin.

> Igor: Well, I'm no longer so afraid to sing bertsos in front of others. They were all older than me. Singing a bertso in itself embarrassed me so... But not so much in high school. I know the other members of the bertso school well, so I don't care about singing badly or well, doing this or that. Knowing my mates better removes that embarrassment about singing in front of your bertso schoolmates [. . .]. That embarrassment, which I had when I started at bertso school my first year of high school.

Practicing bertsos—rhyming and measuring syllables in a particular melody, in addition to singing about a particular topic with another classmate—is practicing taking the floor. One gets to know oneself mind and body. The irregular breathing, the breathlessness, the trembling of legs, the clenching of teeth... can also become manageable as they become familiar sensations. Even if one is not conscious of it, by engaging in the process, one realizes that situations which were once difficult are no longer so. And the process of becoming free of one's embarrassment, and gaining self-confidence, is, for many of the interviewees, a means of self-affirmation.

> Nekane: Oh, well, I'm very shy when I have to speak in front of people, when I have to show my ideas in front of people, very shy... Less so now, but at first I was very scared and even now... The public, in general, is lively,

> and being looked at by them is a big thing. And so I didn't dare to do some things and really improvise... Well, more thanks to bertsolaritza [. . .]. Since then I've really changed and I have dared, and my friends—really good friends now, who at first weren't such good friends—have told me, "It is great what you made since, at first, you used to listen to our conversations but not get involved." And I didn't give my opinions, I didn't say what I felt; and there, I really learned to do it thanks to bertsolaritza and bertso summer camps [. . .]. Then, in life, I'm still shy [. . .], but, yes, I have managed to assert myself a little more thanks to bertsolaritza, and show what I think and who I am, and when I saw a positive reaction to it, I thought, maybe some people won't like me, but I don't care.

For some people, it is the ability to create bertsos in itself that has made them feel this self-confidence. It is a feeling of being capable. The practice itself is a stimulus. As much as the adrenaline of putting themselves to the test, the joy of overcoming the barrier they have set for themselves is appealing. And this has led students to overcome their shyness through bertsos.

> Maiana: Yes, I always have been... I think I was very shy when I was little, and at first everyone used to say to me: "How can such a shy person as you make bertsos?" I don't know, I think I've always had that confidence in myself, if I was doing something I knew I would do well, I don't know. For example, in the first youth championships, you have that adrenaline, you're uncomfortable, but I think it encourages you to do well.

For some others, however, the atmosphere of trust in the team has been a safety net that has encouraged them to take confidence in themselves and to jump.

> Olaia: It's a positive thing [feeling like part of a group]... It has helped me with many things, for example.

> Interviewer: How has it helped you?
>
> Olaia: I don't know. It stops you from getting embarrassed, maybe. Maybe I know myself better. [. . .] I'm more confident in myself [. . .]. Being part of the group makes it a little easier to do things [. . .]. That and the feeling of overcoming fear and shame, to an extent. I think the team helps and gives you strength, and you think "Me too", and there you go… I think it's the team.

Confidence in oneself and confidence in the team are often two sides of the same coin. Bertsos are performed simultaneously individually and in the group. It is this atmosphere of trust that first structures the group feeling between the members of the bertso school, and, therefore, their identification with the group and its members.

Thinking Together

One thinks on one's own as much as one thinks in the group at the bertso school. The process of constructing one's own thoughts is as much collective as it is intimate. And bertso school is not only a place for creativity and enjoyment, but also a place for young people to reflect.

Bertsolaritza itself requires the person who is improvising to be able to look at any given topic from different points of view. And that increases the bertsolari's ability to pass through the sieve of his own gaze instead of uncritically believing in what he has received from others. The characteristic most usually ascribed to oral improvisers, as well as the one being required of them, is critical thinking (Rougier 2016, 3). When making bertsos, one is constantly composing, creating, and receiving discourses, which necessarily requires reflection. In individual work, there is an obvious need to reflect in order to create a discourse: one has to respond to a topic, to put oneself in a certain situation, or to give an opinion. Bertsolaris have to choose what to say and how to say it, and then try to be true to that decision, respecting the bertso's formal limitations. The controversy dynamic created when two bertsolaris interact during the so-called *ofiziotako lana* could be even more interesting. In a state of artificially created dialogue, what Eric Dicharry calls "double décentration intellectuelle" takes place (Dicharry 2013, 65). Driven by a pre-established scenario, the bertsolari has to distance her or himself from her or his usual point of view, speak from a different personality or situation, and take into account the other bertsolari's perspective.

> Kepa: Because that makes us think, the idea I mean, "what would we say there?" and then we have to reflect on it. And we think...And when others sing we also think about their topic, and when they say something it's like, "oh, right!"

Listening to the diverse discourses articulated during the dialectical game structured around a problem, a situation, or a particular event makes oneself think about her or his discursive positions, about what she or he thinks about the topic. And this basically leads to creating one's own ideas and discourses, or questioning existing ones, and then adjusting the discourse or creating new discourses.

> Olaia: I think that helps, you are given a topic, I don't know, well... any topic. And, you have to think about it, and you have to come out with what you think first. And then with another idea... "But, maybe you use that, right?" and "Maybe, well, yes, yes," and then you discuss it, and... listen to it, or... I think that helps us to think a little and to be critical... Either for yourself or about... about other things.

> Uhaina: Bertso school makes you reflect. Maybe about things you wouldn't think about otherwise. I don't know. Hey... You put yourself in other people's place so much, that, in the end, well, at least me... at least it makes me think.

> Maiana: I think intellectuality, [laughter] about everything, but actually… When it comes to talking, the conversations are totally different. We could talk about absolutely anything. It was a very interesting group, and it is everything [...] I don't know how to say it, but the bertso is... This relationship to the reflection; you need to know a thousand things, and on top of that, you have to construct your thinking.

And, in fact, young people explain the impact of shared reflection practices on their own identity.

> Amaia: In ideas and so on, a lot. We often discuss a lot of things, maybe that's where it started, because when we listen to a bertso, we always comment on it, like "what do you think about it?" And well... I don't know, in fact, exactly how, what... But I know it has given me a lot. In regard to relationships and my character.

> Eneka: Bertsos force you to get your brain running, and, in fact, [if I hadn't been to bertso school] I might have been dumber. Maybe.

So, the atmosphere of reflection becomes one of the most important features of bertso school. The capacity for reflection, and the in-depth discussions they take part in at bertso school, distinguishes bertso students from other young people:

> Uhaina: I think bertsolaris… [laughs], well, because I've been in bertsos or since I've been in bertsos, well, I was very young in the beginning, but... It's given me that… The desire to think, and maybe, as you get older, well… I see my thinking and… I associate that desire to think with bertsos. Why, I don't know, but… yes, I link them together. Also because of the people, because you see people who are very thoughtful, very… and because you often have discussions with them that you wouldn't have with other people, or deeper discussions… That's

> why I associate them. I don't know. [. . .] Having a discussion with someone who does bertsos and having a discussion... with someone who doesn't, it's not the same thing.
>
> Olaia: In my classroom, for example, having a discussion, well... I don't know. For example, the other day, "Machismo." What is machismo limited to? Well, my classmates might think, "When a boy hits a girl." And machismo is not that, it's not just that, and... For example, in philosophy class, yes, "the men," but, no! And what about all the others? And so, we said to the teacher and everyone else answered, "Yeah, but, it is one way of putting it!" But we don't have to say it like that just because it's said like that! Well... It is not "the men," and what about "the women?" And so now he says "the humans," well, I mean... Things like that... I don't know, it can be about anything, well... Be it politics, language, life... I don't know.

Another characteristic of bertso schools is that topics that are not mentioned among other people are mentioned there:

> Xabi: Bertsos force you respond to certain topics that you don't necessarily come across in your daily life, and yet you must answer that topic, you know? And, yes, that makes you a little more interested in current affairs or history [. . .] At the age of sixteen or seventeen, thanks to bertso school, I was able to deal with a number of issues, in my head, back and forth, which others of my age had not yet thought about.
>
> Eneka: What did bertsos bring me? I don't know... Those are quite complex things, in fact. I don't know, some values, how can I put it, an awareness about some topics or so, you have to treat very different topics in bertsos. In daily life, for instance, you do not necessarily talk about transsexuals, and nowadays that's mentioned

> in bertsos, well, at least becoming aware that there are issues which are important to some people, thanks to bertsos.

> Kepa: At bertso school and with feelings and... topics... maybe bigger issues, and in setting topics [. . .] they are about everyday society and about life. For example, with my soccer mates, we talk about soccer, sports, and the usual things. And so on. At bertso school, it's more elaborate, more serious.

One can speak about any subject at bertso school because there is an attitude of dialogue, active listening, and trust between the members:

> Allande: Well I'd say... What I'd underline is that I found... People or... I don't know, people who talk about anything. I mean, some issues that I didn't bring up with other friends of my age, there, with bertso friends, I did. But, in a very natural way [. . .]. Well, we still dare to bring up any subject, and I think that's very nice, and we don't have many chances to do that. And you know that your peers will listen to you, and try to understand you, so when you are ready to take on the subjects, it's easier to start talking.

Students are aware that this has led to a process of transformation within them, and in their ideas.

> Eneka: For example, I think I had some values before I started at bertso school. I went deeper into them and discovered new subjects thanks to the bertso school, no doubt about that.

> Kepa: Bertso school changes everything. There is an atmosphere of trust, a good atmosphere, and... it changes ideas and so on.

Moreover, young people understand this tendency to practice thinking as a means of self-knowledge and self-development.

> Jokin: Well, I don't know, you have to come out with what you think, and so in the end you're thinking about what you think, and, I don't know, you have to appear in front of the others, you have to appear somehow, and you have to appear as you are [. . .]. You also notice other things which you might not notice in other situations, and you become aware of how you are [. . .]. You tell your things, you really leave yourself naked... you wonder a lot of questions about your way of being and so on. Then I don't know what I was, so I don't know where I actually was...

They also understand this reflective practice as a way to become a more mature —therefore, not a child anymore— young person, in other words.

> Maiana: I know... that it isn't the same maturity. You can't talk about the same things. With my high school friends, with them... well... I'm not going to talk sitting on a bench... Well, I don't think we would speak about Youth Dynamics[4] and how we feel about the Basque language and the Basque Country, and... no. The situation would be more like: "You watched La Nouvelle Star yesterday," [a TV show] or... Because what we were saying, the friendships you create lead you, in the end, to have more mature conversations and to see many more things in those conversations.

Young people experience bertso school as a place to develop their identity. And they identify with a *young style* as they identify with their peers. Part of that style is thinking,

4 Iparraldeko Gazte Dinamika Berria ('Northern Basque Youth Dynamics') was the name of the process which concluded by founding Aitzina Youth Organization on November 2, 2013.

discussing different topics in depth, and being critical of the world around them.

Activists: We are Capable Because We can, We can Because We are Capable

Bertso school, however, is not something that happens only between four walls once a week. The bertso school community of practice also provides access to areas of socialization beyond itself. Young people at bertso school get into the habit of going to bertso initiatives on their own: they go to parties in different parts of the Basque Country; they stay at their friends' houses; they organize bertso performances; they go to listen to bertso performances. And in this field of socialization, they are used to organizing things to some extent, to divide up tasks within the group, and to drawing up complex plans as a group.

> Amaia: We were going to a bertso performance and, yes, we'll take the bus, and you'll make the banner, and so on, and we made T-shirts to encourage Maiana.

The bertso school, as access to the world of bertso, provides young people with a possible context for organizational training and developing autonomy within the organization. Whether they already have a tendency toward autonomy and commitment beforehand, or whether they develop that when participating in the community of practice, the bertso school allows them —as happens in various youngsters' communities of practice— to detach themselves from home and school adults, and reach for new ways and spaces of socialization.

> Jokin: I think... I would have done this kind of thing if I hadn't been part of the bertso school, but I was motivated to start them earlier than I would have otherwise. For example, when we were in Second grade [at high school], we had the chance to go to Zarautz, I think I didn't know what we were going to do, but we organized it really well, and we had a great time too. And that's

> how we learned to do things like that, we've used it for other things too, we've organized ourselves in that way, and I think that helps because it gives us opportunities [. . .]. Yeah, that's it... I don't know, the first big party in the Southern Basque Country, just between friends, we organized everything without our parents: we went, we slept there, so we got really drunk and met people there... We met new people and, yes, we had a great time, and it was great.

These young people's outstanding characteristic is not only that they socialize through bertso and in the world of bertso. Activism beyond the world of bertso is typical of members of bertso schools. The ability and desire to act and influence, be it in movements for the revitalization of the Basque language, language rights, or political and civil rights, be it in the dynamics of the gaztetxeak [youth centers] in their towns, or the dynamics of high school students.

> Eneka: I don't know why [. . .]. For example, Jokin is part of EHZ,[5] you see people of the bertso schools at the gaztetxe, sometimes half the people at my youth center have gone to bertso school, many of the people in the Baxoa Euskaraz office[6] went to bertso school. There is a need for it. We feel that. Each one, then, is involved not necessarily in the same things, in something they like, but I think there is something. For example, Joanes is

---

5 Euskal Herria Zuzenean (EHZ – 'The Basque Country Live') is an annual three-day music festival. Founded in 1996, it is well-known in the NBC, and is an annual meeting point for young people in the Basque world. It is managed as a non-profit association, and hundreds of volunteers take part in the organization of the festival every year. As a music festival, it promotes clear values and ideas through the ways in which the festival is organized, and through lectures, round-table discussions, and workshops, in addition to the music at the festival. Its ideological focus is on the development of Basque culture and language, the anti-capitalist and alter-globalist struggle, ecology, and sustainable development.

6 As in France, in the NBC you have to pass a university entrance exam which is called Baccalauréat in French and Baxoa in Basque (from Bachot in French). Bernart Etxepare High School students also have to take this exam in French, with the exception of two or three subjects. The Baxoa Euskaraz association, made up mainly of students (but also of teachers) claims the right to take Baxoa entirely in Basque.

> deep into music, Allande's in Aitzina,[7] Amaia has gone on a hunger strike, I think... I'm wondering whether this awareness isn't created before you go to bertso school. 'Cause I think that if you have a connection to Basque maybe you go to bertso school, maybe... In fact, I think it's one of the roots.

The connection is not straightforward or one-way, and, in the words of our interviewees, the relationship between bertso school membership and activism outside the bertso world is complex. But there is a connection. On the one hand, skills acquired at bertso school are useful in other areas: they are able to organize, to have and express ideas, to take the floor and take action. Conversely, what they have learned outside bertso school is also useful for them to apply within bertso school dynamics.

> Amaia: I think we do have strength at bertso school, yes, we have the strength to organize, we have the strength to discuss matters, we have the strength to have fun at such moments; and I think that thanks to that, at high school too we want to get involved with the radio, get involved with things, I don't know... We want to do things and we are able to, moreover, and we are able to move things forward [. . .]. Both things are true, I think... Being in other associations and so on has made that in the bertso school... That's it, the ability to organize, but, in my opinion, at bertso school in particular we learned a lot of things about many situations.
>
> Jokin: Yes, I think so, anyway. Well, above all, that ease to stand in front of people, I don't know if we really have that, but I think that does it, yes. We realize that we are capable of doing other things as well... And others may not be so capable.

7 Aitzina is a left-wing and nationalist youth organization in the NBC, founded on November 2, 2013. The main political tendencies are patriotism and the political left, as well as promoting and defending the Basque language.

It is not just what is learned, but what they feel is useful to them too. The feeling of gaining confidence and surpassing oneself also stands out in the interviews as a key to actively taking part in other groups.

> Eneka: In my opinion, thanks to bertso school you gain confidence, and that confidence may make you feel able to engage more. Trough bertsolaritza, you get further, and you can still get further, engaging. I think we're used to it, maybe, yes. Then, I don't know, I never asked this myself, but I think so; you are committed to something because you know you're able to do it. Then maybe we each do things as best we can, but you know for the same reason that you are worth something, I think.

Also, through activism students have a sense of building a way of being in the world. "Thanks to activism young people gain experience, learn new ideas, get to know people who work for minority languages also. This type of work - in addition to these specific skills - brings them satisfaction and a sense that they have their place in the world" (Dołowy-Rybińska 2016, 428). They develop a way to be young, in other words.

Conclusions

The members of the bertso school have a group identity; together, they give meaning to the experiences they have gone through with one another; and they position themselves together, to some extent, in relation to the world around them. However, this community is structured by characteristics that go beyond bertsolaritza.

> Uhaina: Why do I actually have a good time? Well, because I like bertsolaritza, but you know, along with the people... That's it, there's a complicity between you, and they're like you, so you identify with them right away, and... you have a fantastic relationship with people.

Members of the bertso school have a style that they share, something that the *others* their age do not have.

> Eneka: And there is a certain atmosphere, I know that I only feel that at bertso school, in fact. And, you know, those friends from bertso school, I'm going to automatically connect them with that atmosphere, and, in fact, they're going to be different from my other group of friends, I know that.

They have the ability to take the floor, they can deal with embarrassment, they think critically about the reality around them, and they are committed to changing that reality. And they speak Basque. The members of the bertso school consider these characteristics to be positive, and therefore experience not only their identification with their fellow group members, but also their identity.

> Leire: I think thanks to the bertso school... yes, like, the Pink bertso school, as it has that strength, it makes me feel good, and then, whether it's the bertso school or me… Well… Really, when we are at the bertso school, or in bertso summer camps, or activities related to bertsolaritza, it's me, I am really me, well, I don't know how to put it. And I wasn't like that in middle school; I don't know how to explain… I was, well, I wasn't… I was silent, or… I wasn't saying… it wasn't me, and going to high school, and going to bertso school well, I don't know, you're free, and you think maybe you can be yourself also outside the bertso school [. . .] I think that's bertso… Me, to be myself.

This "me" is, of course, a polyhedron, and one side of that polyhedron is associated with youth identity. In fact, bertso school is also a platform for the young people interviewed to build their youth identity. Loss of shame and gaining confidence are experienced as a process in uncovering one's true self. Thinking together as a way of defining one's own thinking, and as a way of discovering who one is as much as deciding who one wants to be. Students understand taking the floor and engaging in the world of bertso and other spaces as a way to get involved and enjoy themselves as young people. And precisely because they have these characteristics, they have the feeling that they are closer to being young. They have something that makes them more mature, in other words, young adults (Berrio-Otxoa et al. 2003, 83).

> Allande: Yeah, and maybe more maturity; it's not, erm...I don't mean that none of the... the others are mature or anything; some definitely are, but it's true that the bertso workshop crowd, at least I think so, we're quite mature for our age, and you, you can tell.

And this maturity, this process of youth identity construction, develops not only through language practice, but language practice plays a role there too. In addition to bertsolaritza, conversations, parties, dinners, jokes, and debates take place in Basque. If young people build their youth identity through bertso school and bertsolaritza practices, that happens in Basque. The young people's *style* cannot be detached from the Basque language.

> Communities of practice emerge in response to common interest or position, and play an important role in forming their members' participation in, and orientation to, the world around them. It provides an accountable link, therefore, between the individual, the group, and place in the broader social order, and it provides a setting in which linguistic practice emerges as a function of this link. (Eckert 2006, 683)

Two processes of separation take place around the bertso school community of practice: there is the creation of a different style from other young people's, for one thing; and a way of being and doing that differs from adults, for another. And they are attracted to embody their way of being young in Basque precisely because bertso schools and the socialization of the bertsolaritza world symbolize their agency and breaking from adults. For them, speaking in Basque is not simply about obeying what adults have asked them to do. They have chosen to speak in Basque in line with the values of adults, yes, but in their own way. Thus, the rupture is the very condition for there to be no interruption in the continuity of the Basque language.

References

Amorrortu, Estibaliz, Ane Ortega, Itziar Idiazabal, and Andoni Barreña. *Erdaldunen euskararekiko aurreiritziak eta jarrerak*. Gasteiz: Eusko Jaurlaritzaren Argitalpen Zerbitzu Nagusia, 2009.

Baxok, Erramun, Pantxoa Etxegoin, Terexa Lekunberri, Iñaki Martínez de Luna, Larraitz Mendizabal, Igor Ahedo, Xabier Itzaina, and Roldán Jimeno. *Euskal nortasuna eta kultura XXI. mendearen hasieran*. Donostia: Eusko Ikaskuntza, 2007.

Berrio-Otxoa, Kontxesi, Jone Miren Hernández, and Zesar Martínez. *Gaztetxoak eta aisialdia: etorkizuna aurreikusten (2001-2002)*. Gasteiz: Eusko Jaurlaritzaren Argitalpen Zerbitzu Nagusia, 2003.

Dicharry, Eric. *L'écologie de l'éducation: une anthropologie à l'école du bertsularisme en Pays basque*. Paris: Editions L'Harmattan, 2013.

Dołowy-Rybińska, Nicole. "Becoming an Activist: a Self-Representation of Young European Campaigners for Minority Languages." In Wicherkiewicz, Tomasz, et al. (eds.), *Integral strategies for language revitalization*, 405-436. Warsaw: University of Warsaw, 2016.

Duranti, Alessandro. "Agency in language." In Duranti, Alessandro (ed.), *A companion to linguistic anthropology*, 451-473. Blackwell Publishing, 2004.

Eckert, Penelope. "Communities of practice." In Brown, Keith (photos), *Encyclopedia of language and linguistics*, 683-685. Amsterdam: Elsevier Science, 2006.

Eckert, Penelope, and Sally McConnell-Ginet, 1992a. "Think practically and look locally: Language and gender as community-based practice." *Annual review of anthropology* 21: 461-490.

———, 1992b. "Communities of practice: Where language, gender and power all live." In Hall, Kira, Mary Bucholtz, and Birch Moonwomom (eds.), *Locating power: Proceedings of the second Berkeley women and language conference*, 89-99. Berkeley, CA: Berkeley University.

———,1995. "Constructing meaning, constructing selves." In Hall, Kira, and Mary Bucholtz (photos), *Gender articulated: Language and the socially constructed self*, 469-508. Routledge.

Feixa, Carles. *De jóvenes, bandas y tribus*, Barcelona: Ariel (1998).

Hernández, Jone Miren. "Playtime: Gaztetxoak, hizkuntzak eta identitateen adierazpenak." *Soziologiazko Euskal Koadernoak* 16, Gasteiz: Eusko Jaurlaritzaren Argitalpen Zerbitzu Nagusia, 2005.

Jociles Rubio, María Isabel. "La observación participante: ¿consiste en hablar con 'informantes'?." *Quaderns-e de l'Institut Català d'Antropologia* 21(1) (2016): 113-124.

Rougier, Thierry. "Los cantos improvisados por los poetas del Nordeste brasileño: tradición, urbanización, expansión, animación de un territorio." *Europa Bat-Batean Jardunaldiak*, 2016. https://halshs.archives-ouvertes.fr/halshs-01561142/document [Consulted May 14, 2020]

Bertsolaritza in Navarre: From the Past to the Present

Julio Soto Ezkurdia

Julio Soto Ezkurdia was born in Pamplona and currently lives in Gorriti, Navarre. After graduating from San Fermin Ikastola, he earned two MA degrees, one in agricultural engineering, the other in Basque linguistics. He was trained at the Iruñea improvisational poetry school, and in recent years he has worked at the Lekunberri poetry school. He has won the Navarrese Bertsolaritza Championship on five occasions: in 2010, 2011, 2015, 2017, and 2019, and he reached the semi-finals of the Basque National Bertsolaritza Championship three times: in 2009, 2013, and 2017. He has also won awards in verse-writing and poetry at the Iruñea literary contest and has published the booklet Blue Skin (2018). In 2012, with Amets Arzallus, he gave a series of vocal performances at Basque clubs throughout California. In 2016, he participated in the international conference on improvisational poetry, "Europa bat batean," and in 2018 in the "International Poetry Improvisers Tour." A columnist for the newspaper Larrepetit and a teacher of improvisational poetry at several Navarrese schools, he is currently working on a screenplay while producing scripts for the children's TV show, Ene kantak (My Songs).

Abstract

How did I, growing up in Iruñea and in a non-verse environment, come to the world of bertsolaritza (Basque improvisational poetry)? What made this possible? What was the status of Navarrese improvisational poetry at that time? How strong was the bertsolaritza program in state-regulated education? And in the verse schools? What is the current situation? Twenty years ago, I had my first bertso learning experience at the Barañain improvisational poetry school and now I participate in several different poetry programs. Apart from becoming a full-fledged poetry improviser, what else did I learn at the poetry schools? For one thing, poetry schools can become schools of life. In this paper, I will analyze the ways in which teaching at the poetry schools has changed in the last few years and what this has meant for the evolution of bertsolaritza. When I was approached to work as an improvisational poetry school teacher, I worked to communicate fully with the students—to build relationships through poetry. In the Basque improvisational poetry schools, the education is equally important for both student and teacher, as both are given an enhanced awareness of and appreciation for this invaluable part of Basque cultural heritage.

History of Bertsolaritza in Navarre

There is no doubt that the roots of bertsolaritza in Navarre are as old as in other provinces. It is another matter, however, when the first written records date from and how many bertsolaris and bertsos we still know about. There are songs that have survived to the present day, and there is evidence of the existence of poets in Navarre in the eighteenth century (although most of them signed without using their full names—for example, the "Son of Berdabio," whom Mikel Laboa once quoted). Some bertsos which were written but never sung also show that there were poets in Navarre at that time, one example being the bertsos about the Belate robbery.[1]

In Navarre, however, there were no notable Basque chroniclers at that time, nobody like Juan Ignazio Iztueta in Gipuzkoa. In addition to that, one of the greatest setbacks to the Basque language in Navarre took place in the nineteenth century, which made it very difficult to make bertsos and collect them. We know that bertsolaris have been in the province for a very

1 Pablo Joxe Aristorena, *Nafarroako bertsolaritza* (Iruña: Nafarroako Gobernua, Hezkuntza eta Kultura Departamentua, 1992).

long time, but we know few specifics. Anonymity is, therefore, the main feature of the history of bertsolaritza in Navarre.[2]

At the beginning of the twentieth century, the new vigor in the cultural movement in the Basque Country also gave some new energy to Navarrese bertsolaritza. No big names like Txirrita or Pello Errota came up, or Xenpelar or Bilintx before them, but, with the turn of the century, there were names to remember: Axura from Etxalar, Juan Miguel Bera from Zubieta, Pedro Maria Etxarte from Lesaka, Santxo and Jose Maritorena from Amaiur, Trinidad Urtasun from Iruri, and Miel Joakin Barun and Kristobal Beiñes from Leitza.[3]

Whatever the names, it can be said that Navarrese bertsolaritza officially appeared in 1936. Two Bertsolari Days were held in 1935 and 1936 and they have been considered to be the beginning of a renewed bertsolaritza; they were later renamed the Basque Country Bertsolari Championship. Not in the first, but in the second there were also Navarrese bertsolaris; Txirrita won the championship that year. For the final, which took place in Donostia, there were three qualifying sessions, including one in Elizondo (the other two were held in Tolosa and Azpeitia). Ten Navarrese bertsolaris took part at Antxitonea trinquete in Elizondo, but many had not heard of the championship (for example in the Larraun, Imotz, Leitza, and Goizueta areas), and so their bertsolaris were unable to take part. Apparently, there were also those who refused to take part for ideological reasons or writing off the tournament as a novelty. The work which brothers Bittori and Esteban Etxeberria and the young Mariano Izeta carried out in search of bertsolaris is very noteworthy. The ten bertsolaris who took part in the first bertsolari knock-out in the history of bertsolaritza in Navarre were: Mixel Dargaitz from Sara, who lived in Amaiur; Simun Ibarra from Sunbilla; Pedro Ibarra and Juan Ibarra from Ziga; Joxe Mari Mutuberria from Eltzaburu; Juan Felix Iriarte from Irurita; Martzel Larrosa

2 Pablo Joxe Aristorena, *Nafarroako bertsolaritza* (Iruña: Nafarroako Gobernua, Hezkuntza eta Kultura Departamentua, 1992).
3 Aristorena.

and Beltran Sahargun from Banka; Patxi Elorga from Lekaroz; and Jean Harriet from Aldude.[4]

Juan Felix Iriarte took first place. Along with Iriarte, Joxe Mari Mutuberria (who was unable to attend the final in the end), Jean Harriet and Mixel Dargaitz also won a place in the final at Victoria Eugenia theatre in Donostia. This is the topic Basarri gave Iriarte, and the latter's answer:

> Where are you from,
> friend Iriarte?
> Created at Iruri,
> part of Navarre.
> You had me in France
> until almost now,
> and I've worked always
> for our side.[5]

In July of the same year, the war began and bertsolaritza went completely underground, both its improvised and written variants. Bertsolaris were condemned to silence, and when their mouths were silenced, there were no bertsos for bertsolaris to listen to. In Navarre, while local bertsolaritza had been able to show itself thanks to the 1936 championship, the outbreak of the war put it back into a very weak state.[6]

In Elizondo, after the first bertsolari competition in Navarre on January 12, 1936, no similar event was held for another twenty-three years. Bertsolaritza during the post-war years has not been studied in depth; little is known about its role in Navarre. While Upper Navarrese Bertsolaritza had the opportunity to make itself known at the 1936 championship, the war and the post-war period condemned it to the shadows. And not only bertsolaritza: the language, too, suffered a setback during those years due to prohibitions, punishments, and harassment.

In the 1960s, bertsolaritza underwent a great revival, even in Navarre. After the previous Bertsolari Day in 1936, the first bertsolaritza competitions were held in Donostia in 1960,

4 Aristorena.
5 Aristorena.
6 Aristorena.

1962, 1965, and 1967. In order for Navarrese bertsolaris to be able to take part in the main session, Euskaltzaindia, the Royal Academy of the Basque Language, organized regional classification sessions. This happened despite the creation in 1957 of a new "Department for the Basque Language" as part of the Provincial Council of Navarre's Principe de Viana arts institute. The department was responsible for promoting Navarrese bertsolaritza during those years and it organized the 1960, 1961, 1962, 1963, 1964, and 1966 Bertsolari Championships in Navarre, which gave a huge boost to improve poetry in the region. There were both a qualifying round and finals. The finals of the first three years were held in Lesaka, Etxarri Aranatz, and Bera, and the next three at Gaiarre Theatre in Iruñea. With the help of Mariano Izeta, priest Pedro Diez de Ulzurrun went in search of bertsolaris for these new championships in Navarre. Twenty-one bertsolaris was the highest number of participants in these tournaments (1960), and fourteen the lowest (1961). These are some of the bertsolaris who sang during those years: Andres Narbarte "Xalto" (Goizueta, champion in 1960 and 1964); Juan and Bautista Perurena (Goizueta); Anjel Aldaz (Ihaben); Bautista Madariaga (Arantza, champion in 1961); Manuel Iriarte (Arribe); Clemente Ezkurdia (Gorriti); Moises Jaio and Pedro Arrastio (Gaintza); Pedro Narbarte (Arano); Miguel Rekalde (Arruitz); Franzisko Goikoetxea (Madotz); Martin Oreja (Errazkin); Jose Angel Linzoain (Iragi); Urbano Egozkue (Eugi); Pedro Ibarra (Arraioz); Marcos Maritxalar and Mauricio Mitxelena (Lesaka); Miguel Arozamena (Lesaka, champion in 1962, 1963, and 1966); and Joxe Mari Mutuberria (Eltzaburu).[7]

The first session of this new era of tournaments was held in Lekunberri on June 26, 1960. The topic-setter asked, "Well, are there any bertsolaris here?" and gradually the bertsolaris began to climb onto the stage, until there were eleven of them. Andres Narbarte "Xalto" took part in the first greeting:

7 Aristorena.

Let's take first
those of the highest degree,
the mayor and the town council,
bishops, priests, gentlemen;
and now whom we truly love,
the regional parliamentarians,
who have come to listen to the bertsos
along with the rest of us,
thank you, all of you,
may God give us a good afternoon.[8]

Thanks to these tournaments, bertsolaritza underwent a great revival all around the country; it can be said that it came out of the shadows and into the light. But the famous Bertsolari Championship final held on June 11, 1967, at the Atano pelota court in Donostia, was the last of its kind in the sixties. The "Department for the Basque Language" of the Principe de Viana arts institute also stopped organizing competitions in Navarre, and bertsolaritza in the province weakened once again.[9]

Historically, the development of bertsolaritza in Navarre has been closely linked to the competitions that were and are held from time to time; and, as happened between 1936 and 1960, the absence of tournaments from 1966 to 1979 again slowed down the pace of development of the art. The bertsolaris who took part in these competitions were left without continuity.

The 1980s saw the resurgence of bertsolaritza in Navarre. Meanwhile, there were Navarrese bertsolaris who took part in the competitions held in Gipuzkoa, but there were few of these bertsolaris, and at the sessions organized in Navarre the presence of these Navarrese bertsolaris was very limited. Bertsolaris Dionisio Mujika, Kontxi Erro, and Antton Erkizia (all from Lesaka), aware of the decline of bertsolaritza in the province after the last tournament in Navarre held in 1966, decided to organize a competition called Paulo Yantzi, which was first held in 1979. The prize was named after Paulo Yantzi

8 Aristorena.
9 Aristorena.

from Igantzi, who had travelled around the Americas, and that was the beginning of the second revival of bertsolaritza in Navarre. This competition was held for four consecutive years, from 1979 to 1982. Dionisio Mugika was the topic-setter, although the Franciscans of Zamarbide in Errenteria also set topics. That first time, six bertsolaris sang in the final held at the Lesaka pelota court: Brothers Joxe Miguel and Joxe Fermin Argiñarena from Errazkin (the former was the winner); Bautista Madariaga and Juan Perurena (both of whom had sang in the previous championships); Jexux Goñi from Oronoz; and Bittor Elizagoien from Arraioz. The next three seasons were also held in Lesaka. The competition took place over a single day, with an elimination round at noon and the final in the afternoon. In the 1980 championship, bertsolaris from both Upper and Lower Navarre took part. Mixel Xalbador, from Lower Navarre, was the champion at this second tournament. As mentioned above, this championship was a milestone on the new path that Navarrese bertsolaritza would take.[10] Here is a bertso by Joxe Miguel Argiña about the Paulo Yantzi championship:

> To say what the Yantzi
> prizes mean,
> if you want it in a few words,
> I'm going to start by saying:
> the energy of new flowers and
> the revival of many old
> the tree which had fallen ill
> has found its body once more.[11]

At the same time, a very strong and enthusiastic space for Basque language and culture was created in Iruñea. Many people went to the events and courses that were organized, and it was in this context that Eusko Ikaskuntza, the Basque Studies Society, organized the first bertso course in Navarre in 1981. Xabier Amuriza led a group of forty students who started to

10 Aristorena.
11 Aristorena.

get together on Garcia Castañon Street in Iruñea. They had two-hour classes over a dozen Saturdays.[12]

At that time, Amuriza was the bertsolaritza champion of the Basque Country, and it can be said that he was the initiator of modern bertsolaritza. This was true not only because of the innovation brought about by his new verse, melodies, and meter, but also because he was the main founder and agent of bertso schools. Contrary to what had been believed until then, Xabier Amuriza began to defend the idea that bertsolaris are made—that one can learn to improvise bertsos—and, therefore, he developed a method for teaching how to improvise bertsos and established the first bertso schools. That was how the first bertso course in Iruñea came about.[13]

Many of those who enrolled for the course were directly connected with the development of bertsolaritza in Navarre over the following years, people such as Eugenio Arraiza, Lontxo Aburuza, and Mikel Taberna. Many discovered that they were capable of creating bertsos. The course ended with a dinner held at Etxebertze Association in Atarrabia, where everyone ended up singing bertsos and, seeing the success and enthusiasm for bertsos, they decided that the course should be followed up on. This is how the first bertso school in Navarre was founded in 1982. Under the leadership of Lontxo Aburuza, a dozen people began to gather every week at Iruñea's Zaldiko Maldiko Association.[14]

This first bertso school was open from 1982 until the end of the 1990s. After the setting up of bertso schools throughout the Basque Country, and the follow-up to the course given by Xabier Amuriza in the capital of Navarre, the foundation of this bertso school at Zaldiko Maldiko was a very important step in the development of Navarrese Bertsolaritza.[15]

In the early years, the group was made up of some of the students who had taken part in that first course organized by

12 Interview with Lontxo Aburuza. December 20, 2019.
13 Ibid.
14 Ibid.
15 Ibid.

Eusko Ikaskuntza: Mikel Taberna, Mikel Burgi, Juanjo Iturrarte, and Eugenio Arraiza, to name a few. Over time, along with other Navarrese bertsolaris and bertsolaritza enthusiasts (Bittor Elizagoien, Angel Martikorena, and Manu Legarra), people from different parts of the Basque Country—such as Pablo Jose Aristorena, Manu Gomez, Felix Iñurrategi, Mikel Urdangarin, Unai Agirre, the Zeberio brothers, Ricardo Gonzalez de Durana, and Nikolas Izeta—studied bertsos in Iruñea.[16]

While Lontxo Aburuza initially led this bertso school (with the help of Mikel Taberna), in the following years the students took over the leadership of the group; they created and set each other's topics during their Wednesday night meetings. They would first have dinner together, then start singing bertsos.[17]

In this new, exciting context, some of the founders of the Zaldiko Maldiko bertso school decided to reformulate the Paulo Yantzi competition in Lesaka, believing that bertsolaritza in Navarre needed to take another step forward. This championship was an important step to bring Navarrese bertsolaritza back from the shadows and into the light, but it was not enough by itself. Following in the footsteps of these sessions, the Navarrese Bertsolari Championship began in 1983 under that name for the first time. Now, not only bertsolaris from Upper Navarre and Lower Navarre, but also those from the whole of the Northern Basque Country began to take part, until, in 2004, it branched out into two separate competitions: the Navarre Bertsolaris Championship (for Upper Navarre bertsolaris), and Xilaba (for bertsolaris from Zuberoa, Lapurdi, and Lower Navarre). Until 2011, this first tournament had been held every year, but then it was decided to hold it every two years. So, the latest ones were held in 2013, 2015, 2017, and 2019.[18]

This new, more ambitious project also received wider support from bertsolaris. From the thirteen bertsolaris who had taken part in the previous Paulo Yantzi championship, the

16 Ibid.
17 Interview with Bittor Elizagoien. December 18, 2019.
18 Interview with Lontxo Aburuza. December 20, 2019.

number of participants rose to nineteen; and what had been a single-day session now had three qualifiers and a final.[19]

The change in form and direction also led to the founding of the bertso school in Igoa in 1984. At the request of Jon Aleman from Etxaleku, Lontxo Aburuza led the students, and a group of about ten people began to gather in the attic of the village restaurant on Friday nights. It was not as successful or as long-lasting as the bertso school at Zaldiko Maldiko (it was a short-lived project) but setting up a new bertso school was an important step; while in the city people might have been reluctant to study bertsos, this was true even more so in the countryside.[20]

The decisive step came in 1984 with the foundation of the Navarrese Bertsolaris' Friends association. Mariano Izeta was named president, Eugenio Arraiza vice-president, and Lontxo Aburuza secretary. The statutes written for this new association were very useful for the soon-to-be-born Bertsozale Association of the Basque Country. The creation of associations opened new doors for bertsolaritza, both in Navarre and in the rest of the Basque Country.[21]

With the creation of the Navarrese Bertsolaris' Friends association, the opening of tournaments, and the setting up of bertso schools, the next big step was to get bertsolaritza taught at official schools. After several meetings with representatives of the Government of Navarre, and the request of twenty-five state schools and ikastolas to practice bertsolaritza, in 1985 bertsolaritza began to be taught at several schools and ikastolas throughout Navarre. Lontxo Aburuza was in charge of going from school to school, and the Navarrese Bertsolaris' Friends association employed him for that purpose. Four Basque towns (Lesaka, Bera, Leitza and Goizueta) and a Spanish-speaking town (Lizarra) were chosen to undertake this new work. They started with pupils between the ages of ten and fourteen. Given the excellent reception from pupils, the challenge was to spread bertsolaritza to as many schools and ikastolas as possible. In

19 Ibid.
20 Ibid.
21 Ibid.

these first five towns, bertso was taught from September to Christmas, and at the following schools from New Year's to Easter, and from Easter to the end of the school year in the rest. The bertso classes were taught during Basque language classes, with teachers staying in the classroom. The teachers were also offered a voluntary bertso course outside school hours.[22]

With the introduction of bertsolaritza in schools, bertso writing competitions were organized for students, as well as spontaneous bertsolaritza competitions. The latter were held at the Elizondo Sports Center, Berriozar School, and the Prince of Viana Institute.[23] In addition to the young bertsolaris who sang, their classmates also travelled to the sessions by bus. These young people took to bertsolaritza, and in a few years they would be the ones to give the greatest impetus to bertsolaritza in Navarre.

Following in the footsteps of Jon Lopategi, young bertsolaris in Navarre also began to go from school to school performing bertso sessions in front of pupils who were practicing Bertsolaritza. Initially this occurred with bertsolaris from other provinces, but over time it became just the local bertsolaris, who had gained prominence.[24]

In 1986, following the example of the Iruñea and Igoa bertso schools, the Bera bertso school was set up under the tutelage of Jose Fermin Argiñarena.[25] And in the same year, the summer sessions were started with the support of the Government of Navarre. These sessions were made up of two veteran bertsolaris and two young people, and they were generally organized in small towns; there were twenty-one sessions each summer.[26] In addition to spreading the roots of bertsolaritza, bertsolaris from different generations sang together, strengthening the connection and relationships between them.

At the same time, an incredibly successful bertso festival was organized for the autumn at the Gaiarre Theatre in Iruñea;

22 Ibid.
23 Ibid.
24 Ibid.
25 Ibid.
26 Ibid.

the stands were filled to the brim. That same year, a bertso session was organized at the San Miguel cattle fair in Iruñea for the first time. Both of these events were welcomed by bertso enthusiasts. Three or four years later they began to organize Bertso Week in Iruñea (later known as Bertsoaroa).[27]

Once the bertsolaritza sessions finished, young people were given the opportunity to continue practicing bertsolaritza. This led to the proliferation of bertso schools in the 1990s. Manu Gomez and Jose Manuel Oiarzabal were the teachers in Leitza, Arbizu, and Goizueta. In the latter town, in honor of the bertsolari Xalto, they started to organize a championship for young Navarrese bertsolaris in 1991.[28] In the region of Bortziriak, for example, a school was founded in 1990. In the first year, fifteen young people from Arantza and five or six others from Lesaka and Bera signed up, and that is how Manolo Arozena and Bittor Elizagoien began teaching in Arantza on Friday evenings.[29] But the second year, they moved the bertso school to the Arrano Association in Lesaka, where many local young people were encouraged to take part. This bertso school was highly influential in the new era of bertsolaritza in Navarre. Many of the young bertsolaris studied there and went on to help revolutionize local bertsolaritza and greatly impact its quality. The first group included bertsolaris such as Estitxu Arozena, Xabier Silveira, Erika Lagoma, Amaia Telletxea, and Iñigo Olaetxea. A second, large group was soon formed, and many young people who would play a major role in this new movement flourished there, for instance Xabier Terreros, Alaitz Rekondo, Saioa Mitxelena, Jon Abril, Julen Zelaieta, and many others. The first group was taught by Bittor Elizagoien; the second by Manolo Arozena.[30] As we have said, there were many young

27 Ibid.
28 Ibid.
29 Interview with Manolo Arozena. December 18, 2019.
30 Manolo Arozena was brought up in Goizueta and lives in Lesaka. After singing bertsos with friends, he made his debut in the 1988 championship. He won the team championship in 1990 and was champion of Navarre in 1991, 1992, and 1993. Bittor Elizagoien, from Arraioz, sang for the first time at the 1st Paulo Yantzi Competition in 1979, and he was champion of Navarre in 1994 and 1999. These bertsolaris are two of the most popular in Navarre and further afield. They

people who studied at this bertso school and went on to play a major role in public bertsolaritza, and who took qualitative leaps in the championships. For example, Estitxu Arozena won the championship in 1995 and 1998;[31] and Xabier Silveira won in 1997, 2003, 2004, 2005, 2006, 2007, 2009, and 2013; he is the Navarrese bertsolari with the most prizes. Others began studying bertsos and went on to be topic-setters or judges. It is worth mentioning the importance of bertsolaris Manolo Arozena and Bittor Elizagoien in the nineties in Navarre; Estitxu Arozena and Xabier Silveira were among the young people who started performing publicly and, two years later, they became very important Navarrese bertsolaris.

Bertsolaritza began to reach more and more schools, and, as a result, more bertso schools were set up. At the end of 1991, the bertso school in the Baztan region was founded, and, as in Bortziriak, a large group of twenty-five young people gathered at the Elizondo Vocational School under Bittor Elizagoien's tutelage.[32] Bortziriak, Leitza, Sakana, Goizueta, Baztan; all of them very Basque-speaking and very much bertsolaritza towns. The creation of bertso schools was a great step forward, as many of these young people went on to sing in Navarre and the Basque Country over the following years. But taking bertsolaritza to Iruñea and the surrounding area was just as important. In addition to what the Zaldiko Maldiko adults had done, there were bertso schools for young people in Iruñea, Barañain, Txantrea, and Anzoategi in the 1990s.[33]

---

have been very important figures in bertsolaritza in Navarre, both as bertsolaris and for their work in the management of the association.

31 Estitxu Arozena was the first woman to win the Bertsolari Championship of Navarre. This is the farewell she sang as champion in the 1995 final in Leitza:

> Women in bertsolaritza
> have not been taken into account,
> we have only just started
> having our say.
> I will accept the black beret
> as a souvenir here,
> but it's not for me,
> and I will say for whom it is:
> the girls who society's impositions
> cast aside.

32 Interview with Bittor Elizagoien. December 18, 2019.

33 Interview with Estitxu Arozena. December 18, 2019.

Lontxo Aburuza stopped working for the association and was replaced by Joxema Leitza. In 1998, together with Estitxu Arozena and Estitxu Fernandez, they began teaching six-day bertso courses in formal education,[34] and that is how I came into contact with bertsolaritza. Estitxu Arozena came to our classroom, and the then-twelve-year-old boy found out what bertso was.

My Experience

I was born in Iruñea, the capital of Navarre, in 1987. I attended San Fermin Ikastola starting at the age of three.

Our family was not particularly enthusiastic about bertsolaritza. My mother was born in Gorriti, a Basque-speaking town in the Larraun valley in northeastern Navarre. It is a small village of ninety-seven inhabitants,[35] whose daily life is led in Basque, and bertsolaritza is very popular there. Mother brought us up and taught us Basque, gave us both life and language, but I don't remember ever hearing any bertsos with her, or talking about bertsos. We didn't listen to bertsos on the radio in our house, nor did we watch Hitzetik hortzera on Sunday afternoons (a television program that broadcasts bertsos, deeply rooted in the Basque-speaking world, and popular in many homes on Sundays).

My father was born in Irurre, a small village of forty-seven inhabitants in the Lizarra area of Navarre.[36] Basque was lost there in the middle of the eighteenth century, and like the rest of our relatives, my father did not have the chance to learn Basque at home. In recent years, the linguistic situation in Irurre has begun to change: some of the young people there have started going to the ikastola in Lizarra, and some adults to the Basque language school; but my father's generation did not have those opportunities.

34 Ibid.
35 "Gorriti," in *Wikipedia, entziklopedia askea*, July 29, 2021, https://eu.wikipedia.org/w/index.php?title=Gorriti&oldid=8618169.
36 "Irurre," in *Wikipedia, entziklopedia askea*, August 4, 2021, https://eu.wikipedia.org/w/index.php?title=Irurre&oldid=8623220.

Just as we spoke Basque with our mother, we had to speak Spanish with our father. It is true, however, that even though he did not give us the Basque language itself, he did pass on to us, from an early age, his passionate attitude toward it. He has always expressed sadness about not having learned Basque as a child, and therefore he too (together with our mother) was responsible for us being able to learn Basque and being able to live in Basque.

We used to spend our weekends in either Gorriti or Irurre, and in both places we received many customs that are part of Basque culture; but the stays in Gorriti in particular helped us to master the Basque language and strengthen our ties with it. However, it was not until I started improvising bertsos that I found out that Gorriti was a place full of enthusiasm about bertsolaritza. I later learned that it had always been a tradition to invite bertsolaris to the local festivals; but in the 1990s, during my childhood and adolescence, this custom fell into disuse and I did not have the chance to get to know bertsolaris and bertsolaritza firsthand.

Later, I started improvising bertsos and became aware of the bertsolaritza present in my mother's town; it was then that I began to hear bertsos on the radios in farm stables, to hear people reciting old bertsos, and to hear about the bertso sessions that had taken place there over the years. At the same time that I got interested in bertsolaritza, it was revived in Gorriti, and, since then, the habit of bringing bertsolaris to summer festivals has also been revived. Nowadays, another bertso session is also held in the town in the autumn, and when bertso tournaments are held, many people go to them.

With bertsos forgotten in Gorriti, and no interest in bertsos at home, how did I get into the world of bertsolaritza? It was no coincidence in my case: I had heard about bertsolaritza at school, and that had been extremely important for me. I was about twelve years old when Estitxu Arozena and Estitxu Fernandez came to our ikastola to teach a bertso course. It was 1999. The first class took place in our classroom, and I became aware of bertsos for the first time. They gave us a six-day workshop and explained to us what bertsos were. We listened to a few bertsos and wrote our debut couplets (two rhyming bertsos), which I still have tucked away at home. I remember that I was very excited, and that bertsolaritza was a great discovery for me.

At that time, Xabier Irujo was my classroom teacher and English teacher at the same time, and, together with Estitxu Arozena, I owe him a great deal for immersing me in the world of bertsos. When we finished the bertso course and took our next English exam, something very special happened that I will never forget: I finished my exam, and when I went to hand it in to Xabier, he asked me to write a bertso. Thinking he was joking, I put my exam down on the table, but he said no: I had to write a bertso on the last page, and he would not take the exam from me otherwise. Totally surprised, I went back to my place in class, and, as he had requested, I wrote a bertso. I do not remember what I wrote that bertso about, but I do know he asked me to write bertsos in the following exams too, and once I wrote one in English.

Apparently, Estitxu Arozena spoke to Xabier and told him that there were a couple of students in the class who had shown interest and ability for bertsos, and she encouraged us to start at bertso school. That was why Xabier began asking me to write bertsos in my English exams. Along with that, Xabier called my parents to explain the situation, and suggested I start attending bertso school. My parents talked to me, and I said that I would like to start bertso school. Although I do not remember why, I did not attend right away: I began a year after that conversation, along with my classmate Ander, at the bertso school in Barañain, a town close to Iruñea.

Estitxu Arozena was the leader at that bertso school, and she helped me take the first steps in my bertso career. She was my bertso teacher for the next few years, until I started studying bertso with Arkaitz Goikoetxea in Lekunberri—as I do to this day.

After I started improvising, I found out that one of my mother's uncles, Clemente Ezkurdia Barasoain, had been a bertsolari, as had one of her cousins, Martin Goikoetxea Ezkurdia. The former had taken part in most of the Navarrese championships held in the 1960s. The latter, while taking part in his first championship in 1966, had to go to North America as a shepherd, and since then, he has developed his bertsolari instinct and improvised there along with Jexux Goñi, Johnny Curutxet, and others.

The Situation of Bertsolaritza in Navarre When I Started and Today

I started in 2000 at the Barañain bertso school, and we had sessions at Haizea Ikastetxea. Joxema Leitza and Estitxu Arozena, members of the Navarrese Bertsolaris Association, taught bertsolaritza in official education and ran most of the bertso schools.

There were already eleven bertso schools up and running at the time: Bortziriak, Baztan, Basaburua-Ultzama, Goizueta, Sakana, Betelu, Biurdana (Iruñea), Doneztebe, Iruñea, Sunbilla, and Barañain.[37]

It is difficult to know about all of them, as there are always some which get left out of the data, but according to the data received in 2000, approximately 135 sessions were organized in Navarre that year. Most were in Basque-speaking areas, and only a few took place in Iruñea and the Iruñea area.[38]

The situation has changed a lot in the last two decades; Navarrese bertsolaritza is strengthening and expanding its roots. An example of this is the fact that the bertsolaritza program is currently reaching Basque-speaking, as well as towns in which Basque is weaker such as Gares, Lizarra, Zubiri, Garralda, Erronkari, Otsagi, and Agoitz. According to data collected for the 2018/2019 academic year, the program reached forty-two

37 https://bdb.bertsozale.eus
38 Data provided by the Bertsozale Association of Navarre. https://www.bertsozale.eus/eu/nafarroa

towns. A total of 2,900 students, divided into 161 groups, heard about bertsos.[39] Compared to twenty years ago, there has been a significant increase in the number of towns and students involved.

Bertso reaches more areas not only in formal education, but also with regard to bertso schools and bertso sessions. As far as bertso schools are concerned, there has been a significant increase in recent years. There were 11 teams two decades ago, whereas now there are 47 (of these, 32 are aimed at children and young people, and 15 are adult groups—a total of almost 300 students). In formal education, when examining the proliferation of bertso schools in that context, there are different factors to consider: for one thing, there are more and more young people who choose to learn and follow bertso at school; another element is that bertso schools are now set up in non-Basque-speaking areas. Those in the town of Erro, in the Pyrenees, and in Lizarra—as mentioned previously—stand out.[40]

The number of bertso sessions organized in the province has also increased in the same proportion since around 2000. From those 132 sessions, we have moved on to 252 sessions organized in 2016.[41] Many more than that were probably organized, but as mentioned above, data is often incomplete. The Bertsozale Elkartea (Association of Friends of Bertsolaritza) of Navarre supports and organizes some of these, but most of them are organized outside the association—for instance, those held at festivals in different towns, and bertsolari-specific lunches, dinners, and festivals. These are the numbers of bertso sessions organized in Navarre since 2000 (the last two months of 2019 have not been included):

39 Ibid.
40 Ibid.
41 https://bdb.bertsozale.eus

Year	Value
2000	132
2001	132
2002	117
2003	136
2004	184
2005	157
2006	152
2007	171
2008	201
2009	183
2010	200
2011	220
2012	202
2013	186
2014	217
2015	228
2016	252
2017	218
2018	212
2019	200

The association organizes various initiatives and sessions. Among the most notable: [42]

- Navarre Bertsolari Championship. This is held every two years, with 10 regular sessions: a preliminary round, five quarterfinals, three semifinals, and a final. About thirty bertsolaris take part. The last two finals were held at the Iruñea Anaitasuna in front of 1,400 bertsolaritza enthusiasts.
- Bards. This is a group bertso initiative that takes place in years when the tournament is not held. There are groups of at least five people, including three bertsolaris from different categories, a topic-setter, and another member who helps to organize the sessions.
- Navarrese Inter-school Bertsolari Championship. This tournament is organized for young bertsolaris aged 14–18. In the 2019 edition, fifteen young bertsolaris took part.
- Bertsoaroa. This bertso cycle takes place every autumn in Iruñea. There are ten different bertso sessions, and the public's response is enthusiastic. It has become a very

42 Data provided by the Bertsozale Association of Navarre. https://www.bertsozale.eus/eu/nafarroa

successful event. In total, about one thousand listeners come to these sessions, which are held every year.

- Mariano Izeta Bertso Championship. This championship is held for young bertsolaris. In 2018 it was held over three sessions.
- Bertsokabi Championship. This is another youth championship which was organized to replace the Xalto championship. In 2019 it was held over four sessions and 18 bertsolaris took part.

The number of employees working in the Navarrese Bertsolaritza Association has risen significantly, as it has in the bertsolaritza program. While Lontxo Aburuz was the only employee when the association was set up, and Joxema Leitza and Estitxu Arozena did most of the work from the year 2000 onwards, there are currently two administrative workers and six teachers in employment. In addition to that, there are seven other people who teach at bertso schools in different towns. [43]

The Challenges Facing Bertsolaritza in Navarre

Bertsolaritza in Navarre, like in the rest of the Basque Country, has been, is, and will continue to be closely linked to the health of the Basque language. Basque has been severely punished in Navarre for centuries, and it continues to be so today. From being the main language of the region a few centuries ago, our language has suffered considerable setbacks. One need not go very far back in time to when it was forbidden to teach or speak Basque at school: during the war of 1936, and in the long years after the war, Basque children and young people in Navarre had to go to school in Spanish. As did my mother. And not only at school, but also outside of school, speaking Basque was frowned upon. It has always been very clear to pro-Spanish forces that the weakening of the Basque language is a tool to prevent Navarre from starting along other routes, and that is why our language has been and continues to be so severely punished.

43 Ibid.

In 1986, the Law on the Basque Language in Navarre was passed, and it classifies the official status of the Basque language in the region and sets its presence or absence in education and public administration. Due to this law, it is possible to live in Spanish throughout Navarre, but in Basque only in certain areas; it was legally determined that there should be citizens with different rights within the province. The province is divided into three areas:[44]

1) **The Basque-speaking area:** Along with Spanish, this is the only area where Basque is the official language. The right to receive public services in Basque only exists here, as well as Basque being a compulsory school subject. Only nine percent of the population of Navarre lives in this area. Of the population over the age of sixteen in this area, 61% are Basque speakers, another 13% understand Basque, and 25% are monolingual Spanish speakers. [45]
2) **The mixed area:** Basque is not legally official. Education may be provided in Basque, but it is not compulsory. Public administration can be carried out in Basque, but civil servants are not obliged to answer in Basque, and in some cases knowing Basque does not count as a plus in selection procedures for public administration. Sixty-three percent of the population of Navarre lives in this area. Eleven percent of the population over the age of sixteen are Basque speakers, a further 12% understand Basque, and 76% are monolingual Spanish speakers.[46]
3) **The non-Basque-speaking area:** Basque is not legally official and, until 2016, it was impossible to learn Basque in state schools there. Since then, it may be possible if you meet certain conditions, but it is not easy. Place names must be given in Spanish, and Basque has no rights in

44 "Euskararen Foru Legea," in *Wikipedia, entziklopedia askea*, September 23, 2021, https://eu.wikipedia.org/w/index.php?title=Euskararen_Foru_Legea&oldid=8677129.
45 Ibid.
46 "Nafarroa." In *VI. Inkesta soziolinguistikoa 2016*. Eusko Jaurlaritzaren Argitalpen Zerbitzu Nagusia, 2019.

> public administration. Twenty-seven percent of the population of Navarre lives in this area. Of the population over the age of sixteen, 2.7% are Basque speakers, a further 6.8% understand Basque, and 90.5% are monolingual Spanish speakers.[47]

Today, the Basque-language cartoons for children broadcast by ETB 3 cannot be seen in many towns in Navarre, because the channel has not been given a license to broadcast in those areas. Similar examples can be used to describe the difficult situation the Basque language is in.

Two pieces of information about the population of Navarre as a whole that I would like to point out are: 27% of three-year-olds were enrolled in the Basque language school model (Model D) in 2018, and 13% of the population over the age of sixteen (or 69,000 people in Navarre) are Basque speakers. In 1991, only 9.5% of those over sixteen were Basque speakers, a figure that has risen by more than three percentage points in recent years.[48] It is obvious, however, that obstacles created by the law make it impossible for the recovery and strengthening of the Basque language to be any faster or greater. And with weak Basque, strong bertsolaritza is not possible. Improving the situation of the Basque language is, therefore, one of the main keys to bertsolaritza in Navarre, as bertsolaritza needs Basques to sing and listen to bertsolaritza. It is clear that a strengthening of support for the Basque language is needed. The abolition of the 1986 Law would lead to a fresh resurgence of the language, and, therefore, of bertsolaritza.

The Bertsozale Association of Navarre must continue to be strengthened. It has gone from only one employee when it was set up, to now having eight, but it is still very much dependent on decisions taken by the Government of Navarre, and the situation is not easy. The government's financial support and

---

47 Ibid.
48 Ibid.

political will, too, affect the project as well as the bertsolaris themselves.

Having said that, and despite some difficulties, bertsolaritza is in good health in Navarre. We have already examined the data showing increases in official education, bertso schools, and the sessions that are held, and the current trend is also upwards. The challenge, and one of the main keys in the years to come, will be to expand the bertsolaritza network while taking into account the association's possibilities and limitations, hence reaching more young bertsolaris and attracting young people to bertso schools. This will lead to an increase in bertsolaritza in Navarre, along with the number of bertsolaris, and, as a result, there will be more and more bertso sessions.

In addition to holding more bertsolaritza sessions, another challenge moving forward is to hold sessions in places where bertsolaris have not been seen before, or in places where the Basque language, and consequently bertsolaritza, is weak. In general, most bertso sessions are organized in areas where the Basque language prevails. Data from 2018 bears witness to this: of the 209 sessions organized, 189 were in mostly-Basque-speaking areas (Baztan, Bortziriak, Malerreka, Leitzaldea, Goizueta, Arano, Araitz, Larraun, Sakana, Ultzama, and Basaburua) and Iruñea and the surrounding area; 12 were held in the Zangoza area (Aezkoa, Artzibar, Erroibar, Esteribar, the Erronkari Valley, Luzaide, Orreaga, and Zaraiztu); 7 were in the Lizarra area; only one session was organized in the Erriberri area; and none were in Tutera.[49] I have mentioned that the situation of the Basque language differs between some areas of Navarre and others. One direct consequence of this is that bertso sessions are also organized more frequently in certain areas than in others. But bertsolaritza is gradually reaching the non-Basque-speaking areas. It is essential to continue along that route for bertsos to be heard in as many places, and as often, as possible.

This is also the aim of the sessions organized for the Navarrese Bertsolaris Championship: it always tries to hold the

49 Data from the Xenpelar Documentation Centre.

sessions in as many areas of Navarre as possible, and—although there will be fewer bertsolaritza enthusiasts there—that also means non-Basque-speaking towns. Examples of this are the towns chosen during the last three championships: In 2015, Iruñea, Irurtzun, Zubiri, Lizarra, Lakuntza, Berriozar, Lesaka, Burlata, and Elizondo; in 2017, Iruñea, Tafalla, Auritz, Lakuntza, Irurita, Uharte, Bera, Ansoain, and Agoitz; and in 2019, Tudela, Urdax, Irurita, Lizarra, Etxarri-Aranatz, Atarrabia, Lesaka, and Iruñea.[50]

The number of bertsolaris in Navarre is increasing, and with this progress comes another challenge: making a qualitative leap in terms of standards. The work that has been done in recent decades and the qualitative improvements that have been made is substantial, but we must continue in this direction—there is always room for improvement, and there is no lack of enthusiasm or resources.

Quantitatively, too, more has to be done, as the presence of Navarrese female bertsolaris on stage is still scarce. For instance, there were no women in the finals of the last three Bertsolari Championships in Navarre. Of the twenty-four bertsolaris who qualified for the quarterfinals of the last tournament, only six were women. It is true that the data about students at bertso schools is promising: according to the most recent data, there are 268 students in bertso schools in Navarre, 118 of whom are female.[51] So the challenge here is to continue working to identify and eliminate the difficulties for female bertsolaris to start performing in public, to help them in that process, and, as in the rest of the Basque Country, to delve deeper into the gender structure of bertsolaritza and invent ways to lead bertsolaritza in feminist directions.

There is no shortage of challenges, but the path being trod is fruitful, and there is hope that good things are to follow.

---

50 Data provided by the Bertsozale Association of Navarre. https://www.bertsozale.eus/eu/nafarroa

51 Ibid.

References

Aristorena, Pablo Joxe. *Nafarroako bertsolaritza.* Iruña: Nafarroako Gobernua, Hezkuntza eta Kultura Departamentua, 1992.

"Euskararen Foru Legea." In *Wikipedia, entziklopedia askea*, September 23, 2021. https://eu.wikipedia.org/w/index.php?title=Euskararen_Foru_Legea&oldid=8677129.

"Gorriti." In *Wikipedia, entziklopedia askea*, July 29, 2021. https://eu.wikipedia.org/w/index.php?title=Gorriti&oldid=8618169.

"Irurre." In *Wikipedia, entziklopedia askea*, August 4, 2021. https://eu.wikipedia.org/w/index.php?title=Irurre&oldid=8623220.

"Nafarroa." In *VI. Inkesta soziolinguistikoa 2016*. Eusko Jaurlaritzaren Argitalpen Zerbitzu Nagusia, 2019.

Interview with Lontxo Aburuza. Mendillorri, December 20, 2019.

Interview with Estitxu Arozena. Lesaka, December 18, 2019.

Interview with Manolo Arozena. Lesaka, December 18, 2019.

Interview with Bittor Elizagoien. Oronoz-Mugaire, December 18, 2019.

Basque Country Bertsozale Association, 2019.

http://www.euskarabidea.es/fitxategiak/ckfinder/files/NAF-Inkesta%202016%20euskaraz.pdf

Data from the Bertsozale Association of Navarre, 2019. https://www.bertsozale.eus/en/nafarroa

Data from the Xenpelar Documentation Centre, 2019. https://bdb.bertsozale.eus

Learning about Art and the Art of Learning

Maialen Lujanbio

Maialen Lujanbio was born in Hernani, Gipuzkoa. She has an MA in fine arts and has had a long and prosperous career in the world of improvisational poetry. She has been improvising poetry for over twenty-five years. She was the world champion of Basque improvisational poetry in 2009 and 2017. Maialen has participated in several collaborative projects focused on poetry improvisation that have produced a variety of experimental, musical, and radio performances, as well as solo performances that mix singing and reading. She also participates actively in Basque popular media in the Basque language and often collaborates with the Basque newspaper Berria and with Euskadi Irratia, the Basque public radio system.

Abstract

The creation of the bertso-eskolak (improvisational poetry schools) responded to deep social concerns about and awareness of the loss of Basque speakers and the potential loss of bertsolaritza (Basque improvisational poetry). Throughout the twentieth century, the transmission and preservation of bertsolaritza took place largely in rural areas, especially in farmhouses and taverns. In private spaces, improvisational poets were often asked to compose very particular types of poems. In public spaces, they generally performed in a setting that approximated the experience of a group around a table after a meal. Most practitioners were men. As a result of urbanization and the weakening of oral traditions (often due to new technologies and new forms of entertainment), bertsolaritza was under serious threat. However, the tradition is still thriving today as a living phenomenon that attracts young people, both in contemporary, urban settings and more traditional, rural ones. How did bertsolaritza, against all odds, become one of the strongest and most relevant cultural practices in the Basque Country? The first and most important key to understanding this phenomenon is the creation of bertso-eskolak. In these schools, teachers designed a new, "natural" way of transmission and dared to teach "what couldn't be learned."

These lines by bertsolari Joxe Agirre Oranda are well-known:

> Is a bertsolari 'born' or 'made'?
> At least the first time, he/she was born.[1]

One could argue, however (and a bertsolari always has an argument at the ready) that the first bertsolari was "made," through his life experiences, not born that way.

The chicken and the egg debate can go on like a spinning wheel.

Xabier Amuriza created and started the revolutionary idea of bertso schools. It was also his unique answer that disarmed an old belief:

"Is a bertsolari intrinsically so, or can he or she learn?" But the ability to learn is intrinsic too!

An 11-Year-Old Girl at a Bertso School

I heard from our neighbour, a 13-year-old boy, that he had come up with a bertso for the first time. I remember he had rhymed amona—which means grandmother—with komona (bathroom). He had thought it up at his school's bertso school. I didn't even know there was a bertso school. I probably didn't even know you could write bertsos. I didn't know anything at

1 Cited by Joxemari Iriondo and Antton Haranburu, "Bertsolaritza gaur eta bihar," *Jakin*, no. 14–15 (1980): 38–49.

all about bertsolaritza. It turns out, some of the songs I learned at school were, in fact, bertsos.

I listened to our neighbour's bertso, and the next day or so I remember composing something resembling a bertso in my head. That bertso came to me, to my 11-year-old mind. I remember that it was about my classmates, and that it had the oldest, the most energetic, the fastest, and the best rhymes.

It was circa 1987. Bertso schools had only been around for a few years at schools, dotted around the region. Meanwhile, it was up to Basque teachers and bertsolaris to decide whether or not to set up bertso schools; it depended on their desire to do so. Bertsolaritza was not an official subject, and it wasn't part of the curriculum. It was an extra-curricular activity and depended mostly on each teacher's commitment.

There was a bertso school at our school. Our teacher, seeing that we were messing around with bertsos, suggested that three classmates attend. That's how we started, us three youngsters, along with some older kids. I was the only little girl.

I started unexpectedly, and I've never stopped. Even though, paradoxically, rarely did I actually go to bertso school.

What drew that 11-year-old girl to bertso school? Doing it. Doing it myself. Coming up with the bertso myself. Being able to say it. That brought me to bertso school. I didn't know much about the bertso world, I didn't have any aims, I wasn't dreaming of becoming a bertsolari, I didn't have an objective. Doing it, and enjoying doing it: that's all I cared about. That's all. I wasn't attracted to the bertso world, but to bertsos themselves. To coming up with bertsos.

Male 30-35: "Enjoyment is a very important feature, and everything else stems from enjoyment. Young people aren't attracted to cultural projects because of their values and messages. That counts too, but young people like having fun, and that's what makes them want to increase their knowledge; becoming a bertsolari because of wanting to know more, wanting to find out about history, wanting to find out about and understand the movement, to want to take part."[2]

So we started at bertso school. Outside of class time, once a week, we would get together in the dining area at midday. The smell of burnt potato omelette in the air. It was a small group: three, four, or five of us. A special group. We were doing something unlike anyone else. Bertsolaritza.

Me, I was a fan of singing; I loved playing with language and writing stories, but I didn't know much about what the activity really was.

Bertso School: Excavating in the Air[3]

Pello Errotak: *Ari naizela, ari naizela,* *hor ikusten det Txirrita.* *Eta zein ez da harrituko gaur* *gizon hori ikusita?* *Dudarik gabe egina dio* *andregaiari bisita.* *Oso dotore etorri zaigu* *bi alkandora jantzita.*	Txirritak: *Hauxe da lotsa eman didana* *gizon artera sartuta!* *Edozer gauza esaten degu* *edanarekin poztuta.* *Bi alkandora ekarri ditut,* *bat eranztea ahaztuta...* *Pellok bi nola jantziko ditu* *bat besterikan ez du ta?*
Pello Errota: I'm doing it, I'm doing it, I see Txirrita there. And who won't be amazed to see that man today? There's no doubt he's gone to see his fiancée. He looks very smart to us with his two shirts on.	Txirrita: That's what's embarrassed me, being among men. We say anything when we're happily drinking. I'm wearing two shirts, one of them I'd forgotten to take off. How could Pello wear two shirts when he only owns one?[4]

2 Harkaitz Zubiri Retortillo, Alfredo and Xabier Aierdi Urraza, Kultura ez da at-batekoa: bertsolaritza aztergai (Bilbao: Universidad del País Vasco/Euskal Herriko Unibertsitatea, 2019).

3 "Ari naizela." Pello Errota and Txirrita.

4 This is an old conversation between two bertsolaris, Pello Errota and Txirrita. Bertsos, italicized in this work, have been translated into prose to give an idea of

It was typical to sing old bertsos, like the one above, at bertso school. This practice was for a reason. Singing old bertsos opened something up. Something from the past into the present. We learned melodies from those bertsos. Through melodies, we took in metrics without realizing it. Not only did we learn the logic of rhymes, but rhyme combinations as well. We took in the stories and styles of bertsos from the past. Language's nooks and crannies, poetic changes in sentence order, and special ways of saying things.

Old bertsos nourished us, trained our memories, fed our understanding, helped us practice and imitate. Unconsciously, we began to understand the logic of the rhymes through melody. In the old bertsos, there was knowledge of tradition as well as a pattern, language, and emotional attachment to that world. Pleasure through singing. Singing itself was a pleasure, and singing aloud and together forged a strong, intimate connection.

But hey! Those bertsos, those ideas and rhymes, those tunes, they had internal structures!.

Pello Errotak:	*Zortziko handia:
Ari naizela, ari naizela,	______/______ 10
hor ikusten det Txirrita.	______ (errima) 8
Eta zein ez da harrituko gaur	______/______ 10
gizon hori ikusita?	______ (errima) 8
Dudarik gabe egina dio	______/______ 10
andregaiari bisita.	______ (errima) 8
Oso dotore etorri zaigu	______/______ 10
bi alkandora jantzita.	______ jantzita. 8
	(bukaera)

[errima = rhyme; bukaera = end]
* Zortziko handia = A rhyming pattern used in bertsolaritza. (Literally, the big eight.)

their meanings; the rhymes have not been reproduced in translation (translator's note).

The internal logic of bertsolaritza was something you became aware of at bertso school; the composition of bertsos. At bertso school we excavated the melodies and discovered the tunes' skeletons:

The mystery had a technique behind it, a recipe. So anyone could try it.

We started writing on paper in slow motion, writing, then singing out bertsos aloud.

Think of the idea for the end first and write it down.

Put that idea into the metric. At first, we counted the syllables on our fingers.

Follow the rhyme at the end to look for more rhymes from bottom to top. Write a short list at the end of the paper and choose from it.

Arrange a sentence to go with each rhyme. A suitable idea to go with each topic. Put them into the metrics as well. Make sure they bond together.

And so, from bottom to top, the bertso comes together on a sheet of paper with writing all over it.

Written from the bottom up, it had to be sung from top to bottom.

We worked on our bertsos like this:

Rhymes

We made short lists, even with words we hadn't heard before. I first heard the words attention, numerous, and martingale at bertso school. We needed the greatest possible knowledge of the language to have the widest pool of rhyming options. And our taste for language awoke there, along with the need to start handling language like clay.

Metre: Small Zortziko (7/6 7/6 7/6 7/6).
Big Zortziko (10/8 10/8 10/8 10/8)

If a lot had too few syllables, then you could say it was a whole lot. Several, too, or so many, or even a hell of a lot. As many syllables as the metre required. The strict requirements of metrics meant we needed language resources. That's what the never-ending game was all about: Pull on the dough of words, gather the dough of words up.

________________ 7 ___________6 ________________ 7 ___________6 ________________ 7 ___________6 ________________ 7 ___________6	*Asko izaten dira* ___________7 *Hainbat izaten dira* _________ 7 *Hainbeste izaten da* _______ 7 *Makina bat badira* __________ 7 *Amakina bat bada* __________7 *Horrenbeste izanik* __________7

Expressions

We had to find a way to convey messages. A bertso never contained a flat word. It was a poeticized record, or something "versed." You had to learn to bend and twist the language in order to make it fit, to say what the words could and then make them say more.

Ez irudiyan hark kabiyari *beste zulo bat atzian* *egiten diyo handik sartzeko* *aurrekua tapatzian* *erakustiaz pentsa zagula* *nundik atera sartzian*	*Nik neska-zahar bat eskatzen dizut* *egongo zera jakinda* *baino zahrrikan ez badaukazu* *gaztia ere berdin da.*

Values

A type of ethics or morals. As bertsolaris have been considered the "voice of the people," they tend to have a critical approach. In favor of the weak, and against power. This comes across in old bertsos and in new ones too.

<table>
<tr><td>Sermoi ederrak aditu arren
ez dira asko estutzen,
lapur txikiyak preso sartuta
berak milloiak ostutzen.</td><td>juezak alde daukazkiyenak
irabazten du auziya,(...) aundi
gaxtuak nai duen arte
txiki onaren biziya.</td></tr>
</table>

Meaning and Patterns

Bertsos weren't verbal, they weren't written poetry. The intonation, the musicality of reason: that was what we took in. If those ways of saying things have lasted for years, it is because they are effective; they are patterns with expressive strength. Always good for reusing.

<table>
<tr><td>Animaliyen artian ere
lapur aundiya nagusi.</td><td>Alper askori gustatzen zaio
bestek egiña jatia</td></tr>
</table>

Formulas

Formulas are powerful, repeatable patterns that can take on a thousand different meanings.

<table>
<tr><td>Ni bezelako gizon batentzat
ez ote da zoritxarra,
itsasoa hain hurbil izan da
ohean egon beharra. 3

Poz bat bakarrik daukat
bizitzan
Franco ez nula serbitu. (bis)3</td><td>________________ 10
ez ote da zoritxarra 8
__________________ 10
_________ beharra 8

Poz bat bakarrik daukat
bizitzan 10
_______________ 8</td></tr>
</table>

Bertsolaris use poetic, rhetorical strategies. Take, for example, the effectiveness of the paradox, "You have one child, your wife two." There is also the strength of repetition: "Three clocks, three chains each, each with three levels." And many others. Instinctively and unnamed, a world appears in the melodies of the bertsos—just as mist rises up off the sea.

There wasn't much learning material when we started. Three or four people, each with our own notebook, and a few photocopies to fill in the gaps. From there on, we had to make it all up.

Making bertsos by writing them on paper, we started working on the muscles in our heads. Molding the clay that is language. Turning a 14-syllable sentence into one of ten. Shaping the dough in your head, writing it down so you didn't forget it, reshaping it, correcting it on paper. Continuously thinking, writing, and gradually ... Homo erectus. Young bertsolaris began to rise up from the paper.

Adapting syllables to fit the tune, remembering the rhymes, and singing a bertso aloud a minute or two after coming up with it in your head. Without any notes to rely on, hands in your pockets, and your terrified voice.

Bertso School: Bertsos and within

Bertso schools had and still have some special features specific to them, not included in other activities for young people.

Each bertso has its own time and place. Each has its own words. And they will all be heard.

Making bertsos is just as much about learning to listen as it is about learning to speak, because you have to respond to what the other bertsolari tells you. Also because the other person is singing, out there all alone, and deserves your attention and respect.

Nudity

Spontaneity is being naked. Spontaneity brings difficult conditions with it: timing, text, ideas, etc. Writing verses, like writing poetry or producing any creative art form, is like stripping naked. Explaining things in your own way.

Maybe because the difficulty is the same for everyone—or because we have all gone through the same anxiety—we value each other more. Especially at bertso school.

Bertso school breaks down or shifts the conventional hierarchies between young people: academic ability, athletic ability, conventional beauty, etc.

The keys to bertsolaritza—ingenuity, sense of humour, ideas, in-depth reflection, originality, etc.—are unique, unimaginable, vague, and non-standard. Unusualness can be a differentiating factor in bertsos. Because there is nothing certain about bertsos. We are naked, and in a sense we are free. Nudity puts us all on the same level.

I would go as far as to say bertso school has been, and continues to be, a more equal playing field than the rest of the world.

The Ability to Think and Reason

Bertso schools and bertsolaritza make you carry out a demanding exercise: Thinking. That doesn't happen in many other activities. Playing different roles in dialectics. Singing from different places.

Perhaps because of this demand, this need to reason, people with different opinions have found ways to work in groups at bertso schools.

Bertso is Code

What is said in bertso must be answered in bertso. Almost anything can be said in bertso, even what cannot be said in words. And it can be said even more sharply, smoothly, strongly, beautifully than in words. That, too, is why it is a fine tool for young people. To deal with love or anger. For lyricism or criticism. Everyone's words are the clothing and hiding place of poetry. And that's no small deal during adolescence.

Bertso is a means of expression: it's viable, cheap, and accessible. Just as early punk was and as hip-hop and rap can be.

Rigid Code could be Suffocating for Some

Bertso schools are enjoyable, egalitarian places. That's why they made room for young girls, too, from the start. But bertsolaritza had and still has its own ways, its rigid codes. A compact body, a strong presence, and a loud voice. Confidence in the word, self-confidence. The ability to create humour, and the belief that you have that ability.

And these forms, these traditions of 'great' bertsolaritza, are more difficult for people with particular origins, bodies, and ways of singing. For girls in general, these codes can be stifling. Although bertso schools have given girls a place, the jump to performing in public (for girls) highlights the old patterns of bertsolaritza.[5]

Bertso School: Bertso and Beyond

A TEAM existed and it still does. We had the feeling that we were part of a special group. At the time, although it wasn't very prestigious (while nowadays it is held in very high esteem), it was our favorite activity. Language, singing, tradition, creativity: we had love, interest, and passion for all of it. Even though we didn't know how to say it, all of that was within us already.

Allure is a necessary pillar to socializing the arts. If it isn't cool, it won't work. That said, there can be many reasons for putting the work in, not just a varnish of coolness. In any case, the discourse of ethics ("you should do this, that and the other …") is not enough. And the most effective of all achievements, and in itself the most sensible and consistent, is to try to combine both discourses: it is beautiful to be here, I have fun, it satisfies me, it moves something inside me, and so I feel good. Bertsolaritza sometimes achieves this, and that is its greatest achievement.

CHAIN of TRANSMISSION: Young adults were young people's teachers. And the young people taught children. This intergenerational connection created an attachment to methodology and formal knowledge which was scarce at the time. Identification with the group, and consequently with

5 Maialen Lujanbio, "As the Tree Grows, the Bark Cracks," in *Female Improvisational Poets: Challenges and Achievements in the Twentieth Century*, ed. Xabier Irujo and Iñaki Arrieta Baro (Center for Basque Studies, University of Nevada, Reno, 2019).

bertsolaritza. Enjoyment and fun. Children and adults came together in bertsolaritza, but also at dinners and sessions at local festivals. There was a deep emotional side to it.

NON-REGULATED: Bertso schools were quite anarchic. They were not regulated at all. They were not formal. Back then, there was nothing you could call methodology. Some photocopies to fill in the blanks, collections of old bertsos ... Apart from that, instructors' work was based on the young people's enthusiasm, passion, and experience. We took it day to day. We spent more time playing than working: playing handball, talking, and eating sunflower seeds. That was also a key part of becoming enthusiasts. All of that, too, was part of making the team; it made bertsolaritza special.

This anarchic and non-formal nature was key to my experience.

Bertsolaritza does have something in common with punk: the do-it-yourself attitude. Although very different sociologically, it was basically raw material, like in PUNK: "it was easy, it was cheap, it was straightforward. It's within reach and we'll take it."[6]

NETWORKING: Inter-school tournaments were organized for young people. We met people we shared interests with from all over the Basque Country. We went from school to school, singing. We saw villages that our classmates hadn't been to. We were members of a rather peripheral, private network. Part of a beautiful community.

And that offered us a different type of adolescence.

Male 30-35: (73): "... they built an atmosphere for us (...) That is where an important phase begins: I had friends all over Bizkaia, which is going to Berriatua or Igorre and having friends there. Organizing a session for a friend, going there, telling people at home that you're going to sleep over there,

---

6 Josu Zabala. "Postgraduate in the Transmission of Basque Culture." 2008. HuHezi

partying, taking part in celebrations (...) there too, on the way out to life, bertso was the journey of initiation."[7]

LOCAL STAKEHOLDERS: Local bertso groups were not and are not (only) greenhouses for bertsolaris. These bertso groups organize local sessions. They run bertso schools for adults and for children. Groups of people who sing at neighbourhood festivities; those who find volunteers to help run the tournament; topic-setters and judges; and schools that educate bertsolaris and listeners with critical appreciation. All these people are active in and affected by local initiatives, arts activities, and Basque language work. At bertso schools, doing bertsos is almost the least important thing.

It is essential to socialize with people in a particular field if you are going to become enthusiastic about it ... Enthusiasm is about soaking up what you are offered, and, to do that, you have to integrate that cultural offering into one of your most effective social experiences. That happens especially during enriching interactions with people who mean a lot to us.[8]

"Natural" transmission was "designed" at bertso schools, and what was later called "socialization" took place:

> Amuriza's theoretical and practical contribution was a fortunate milestone ... in two senses because the revolutionary [the idea and setting up of bertso schools] brings with it the idea of socialization, because there is no other way to guarantee transmission if it is not based on socialization.[9]

Individuals and a Group: Tight-knit, But Not a Herd

> Gehiegi uste izan gabe
> baina garenaren jabe
> gure ideia ta ahots,

7 Zubiri and Aierdi Urraza, *Kultura ez da bat-batekoa*, 73.
8 Zubiri and Aierdi Urraza, 67.
9 Zubiri and Aierdi Urraza, 69.

kaixo denoi! hemen gaude!
(...)
herri hau trinko egin nahiz;
'trinko' diot, ez artalde;
gu ere hala baikara
bakarkako eta talde.[10]

Individuals

Those which form a practising community share an interest in something, learn from each other, and become members of the community by participating (Lave & Wenger, 1991).

Bertsolaritza created such spaces for socialization four decades ago, and thousands of people have already passed through them. This is perhaps the most inspiring thing that the bertsolaritza social movement has created and achieved. They are socialization areas for immersion in the activity. Otherwise, it would be unlikely that so many children and teenagers would become enthusiastic about bertso.[11]

Bertso schools used to be schools without teachers. We only had one adult instructor for two school years. Then there was the village bertso school: a group meeting. Start singing and keep going. Directed by everyone and no one. Singing individually. Always singing in a group.

For me, the group factor has been essential in bertsolaritza. In fact, bertso school was primarily that for me and that is what it is: a group of friends who share an enthusiasm. I didn't study bertsolaritza at bertso school. I did learn about the basics there, but later on it was the context and bertso culture. I didn't go to bertso school every week. I tried to sing as little as possible when I went.[12]

10 2017ko Txapelketako finala. BEC. Barakaldo. Maialen Lujanbio. Hasierako agurra.
11 Zubiri and Aierdi Urraza, *Kultura ez da bat-batekoa*, 69.
12 Lujanbio, "As the Tree Grows, the Bark Cracks."

Bertsolaritza in bertsolari groups

Bertsolaritza, an individual creation, is also a group creation. Everyone creates their own bertsos, but in conversation with another person. That other person's creation affects yours, and yours affects theirs—both the topic-setters' and, in particular, your fellow bertsolaris'. It is a combined form of creation: I and We are both creators at the same time.

That is the key to bertsolaritza: the need for the other bertsolari. You can't do it alone, and that means making sure you have healthy relationships.

In the sessions, each bertsolari takes responsibility for their own work and the group's work. Each bertso session is the responsibility of all the participants. Even if you do not perform as well as you would have liked, the overall outcome of the session is what matters most. The joy of the group, and its intimate bitterness, is often the feeling that comes home.

The very essence of creation is also often shared: it is common to hear a topic and share your idea with the other participants. Also, in the session itself, those left sitting down will share their ideas with the bertsolari who is going to sing. No copyright is charged.

Being such a simple activity, just words, yet so risky in themselves, it inevitably leads us to hold onto each other. Without denying each person's ego, their desire to carry on, or their search for individual brilliance.

The artist in collaboration

The artists' egos, desires, and need for freedom often clash with group directions, projects, and militancy.

In bertsolaritza, you can be an author and a member of an association in a relatively healthy way. Bertsolaritza has organized itself like few other artistic activities: working around an association. Those who viewed bertsolaritza as a cultural movement rather than as an artist's way of making ends meet were quite the visionaries. One of the most significant points of this visionary ability was the transition in 1996 from being the Bertsolari Association (originally founded in 1985) to becoming the Association of Friends of Bertsolaritza, or bertso fans (bertsozale). In other words, we are an association of not only authors/performers, but also fans and organizers and all those close to us.

Today, most bertsolaris are active members of the Bertsozale Association, and many of them actively contribute to it.

Bertsolaritza is not only an artistic activity. Bertsolaris and fans have a mission, and that is to make bertsolaritza last; to indirectly strengthen the Basque language and nurture Basque culture; to cultivate one's own symbolic cultural knowledge; and to enrich the life of an entire linguistic community. Awareness that the group's mission could go beyond artistic creation gives bertsolaris insight beyond their ego, and turns an individual artist (being, in fact, an individual artist) into a group artist (too). I and We. Tight knit but not a herd.

And there we were, Homo erectus, young potential bertsolaris, on our way up.

Baggy Trousers for Improvisation

Young people learn to imitate. Imitation is the most basic learning strategy in all walks of life. This applies to bertsolaritza too.

Creativity is also continual variation; it's that little bit you add to what has already arrived. Bertsos have a repetitive form: their formulas, their language, their few words, and their discourses are renewed in endless combinations, recreating creativity in that way.

By making other people's bertsos our own, by memorizing, by reproducing—that's how the process of learning begins. These verses by other people have a melody (the melody is learned), internal rhythm (the metric is internalized), effective and powerful expressions (language features are worked on), and reasoning (bertsolaris work on tone, coherent arguments, a way of giving ideas substance, and chemical-linguistic composition).

Bertsolaris have a particular posture: their hands in their pockets, a loud voice. Young bertsolaris also study these aspects of bertsolaritza, unconsciously, by imitation.

We, once young bertsolaris, learned by imitating "the others." Those "others"—the bertsolaris—were mostly adult men from the traditional world.

Young children at bertso schools are also given heavy topics. People ask for an opinion, a position, whether it be superficial or profound. Young bertsolaris introduce their words in the formats, melodies, and expressions they have learned, which are more substantial than their own words. Bertsos in pants one size too big.

Young bertsolaris use arguments which don't fit in with their worldview: considerable, heavyweight arguments. That is how they learn to compose and sing bertsos. How they learn to sing with confidence. How they inadvertently adapt expressions in a particular way. How they unintentionally take strong positions on issues. By imitation.

Over time, these internalized perspectives can become ones you don't agree with. Listening to your voice, you hear yourself saying things you don't actually think. As though the words came of their own accord—like the past, like inertia, like the habit of imitation.

Who hasn't caught themselves saying things they don't mean!

It's like that for me at home too,
three or more children.[13]

and

... you have a child
your lady two ...

its echo ...

13 2005-12-18 Barakaldo Tournament 11:00 [Bertsoa] / Unai Iturriaga, Maialen Lujanbio

That's where unlearning comes in. Realizing. Correcting. Once you have internalized the mechanics of imitation, you can begin to use them to your advantage. That's when you start making clothes your own size. Each body type has its own clothes. Because not everyone is at ease in baggy trousers.

"I didn't learn bertsos at bertso school. Only the absolute basics, but after that ..."

School of Intuition

Imitation is a bit like wearing someone else's trousers. Ironed trousers, oversized trousers, but always trousers...

The individual work of each bertsolari begins at the school of intuition. Private. Intimate. You do everything without knowing how to do it. It's even less methodical than bertso school. Everyone comes up with their own learning process.

Fortunately, bertsolaritza is not a sport, it isn't a music conservatory. We don't know how much one needs to train the day before, what one's pulse should be, what to eat, or how much stretching to do to be at one's very best. The same keys don't always produce the same sound in bertsos. There is no formula. Fortunately.

How do you "train" to give an answer to your ideological and aesthetic concerns at a moment's notice? And to work on your hang-ups and weaknesses? I don't know. I doubt if anyone does. Everyone organizes themselves in their own way. Everyone looks inside themselves.

Inward to go outward again.

A bertsolari's individual work is not, in fact, individual. Each person's efforts and work have to be put to the test in front of the audience. One's own offering has to be negotiated with the listeners. Not everything is exact; it's a continuous, imperfect search. It's a tug-of-war between what you want to do and what you can do, what people expect and what they are willing to accept. A mutual education. Colliding. Unintelligible. The unintelligible gradually becomes comprehensible. A new path of communication, through bertso, can be opened up over time.

Bertso school gives you the basics. Metre and rhyme. Flour and water. But from a particular moment onward—or side by side, or backward—your own personal work begins:

Looking for opinions which are more yours. Fleeing from the echo of that voice that you swallowed from tradition. Acquiring old expressive resources and coming up with new things to say with them. Making new waves using the old pattern. Unlearning. Reinventing.

You start going from side to side, looking for the right language that fits in with you and your listeners' reality: comparisons, metaphorical figures, the world of reference … Trying to be contemporary. Or trying to adapt to the place.

Trying out other forms of reasoning, seeing whether they are effective, whether they are valid, whether what you want to say is understood …

And opening up another set of topics. Which topic is worth bringing up? And where? Saying what is needed (and not what needs to be said); thinking about what you "need" before you say it.

As times change, you need to represent different characters. Giving a voice to realities and people who have had no place in bertsolaritza; not even being familiar with their voices. The thin thread is improvisation, being in front of people. A microphone and the word are a great opportunity and a risk.

How to sing about pain, for instance, about others' pain without using that to benefit your art. The politically correct is in continual mutation. And there is no humour in being correct. But humour, when it puts down other people, isn't funny. How do you deactivate jokes that are too easy and too popular for easy success, and which can cause pain? When you hear them, you react using irony. And even more when they slip off your own tongue.

You constantly think about your opinions, and your position about the world. And about your task in the session. Whether to give the audience what they want: when you should, when you shouldn't. Why you should, why you shouldn't. Just as long as you don't have to say what you don't want to.

It's hard, delicate. You are in constant contradiction; constantly trying things out and adapting. Spontaneity is continual desire and impossibility.

And you want to provoke your imagination, supply fiction while making references ...

And create language registers for your characters ... Working on the Basque language itself all the time, renewing it and feeding it from the past.

And enriching your bank of rhymes.

And your voice: one of your few and often forgotten instruments. How to get to know and nurture your own voice as you move forward.

And melodies for your voice. Which new tunes do you offer? Which old tunes to bring back? What do tunes from the world of music bring, and what do they take away? How do they make your singing easier? And what about traditional bertso melodies?

And how do you make all that credible? Credibility—that vague and subjective thing. How do you achieve that? Be honest with yourself.

The word. Your word. Your opinion. Your point of view. The gift for your bertsos. Ingenuity. Rigor. Depth. Humorousness. Magnetism. Communication skills. Everything in your voice. Your voice in your body. The way you hold your body. Your body in front of people. You with your fellow bertsolaris. Your whole vehicle in movement. Today, at a certain time and place.

And in addition to bertsos, crowds are needed, and having conversations, talking about topics which are of interest and others which are not; spending hours with people you feel close to and distant from. And trying to enjoy it. An anthropological, sociological, linguistic, cultural activity. Always with people. That, too, is bertsolaritza. In fact, that's the main thing ... The bertso is everything—the words themselves and everything apart from them. Learning about the environment, becoming one with the environment. Studying all the time.

"It's a wise person who knows where they are," said Lazkao Txiki. Those are things you learn in the school of experience ...

Bertsolaritza is expanding into new areas. Communication has to be achieved with all kinds of people from various walks of life. The group of bertsolaris is changing. Their origins, tastes, cultural backgrounds. Society itself, the political and social situation, values ... Everything is changing. And bertsolaris need to know and sing about variations in their surroundings. And those surroundings also change bertsolaritza. Inside and out.

Inside and Out

Listeners are no longer a homogeneous group, large-scale consensus a thing of the past. Topics that used to warm the heart—language, people, freedom—have become more nuanced, more heterogeneous, more liquid, if you will, even within the "wonder" of the Basque world. It's harder to be completely successful and get everyone's approval. More difficult, and therefore more interesting in terms of creativity.

The tempo of society has also accelerated. Few people have the patience to listen. Few people develop the art of saying, enjoying the words and silences of the narrative.

In the past, speeches and bertsos, without being very advanced in terms of narrative or content, could go on for hours. Talking about how robins jump, for example. Saying things this way and that. Narration, ellipses, description. Everything was in the pleasure of using the language itself. Turn in turn, the sweetness of handling the language, the many ways of bending it, the beauty of consonance.

Our world is not what it was back then. Now narratives are over quickly and are full of onomatopoeia. We have swallowed other worlds of education and reference: television, films, tv series, video games, literature. Those many types of narratives have made us who we are. Today's world has new methods of storytelling and a wider variety of topics. In a single bertso, the narrative progresses tremendously, and three bertsos need to cover a whole world to be successful.

Not only the tempo of society, also the socio-linguistic situation of the Basque Country plays a part in the changes in bertsolaritza. Knowledge of Basque is more widespread in the Basque Country, but its use and people's ability to express themselves in Basque is in decline.

What place does the plasticity, beauty, enjoyment of the Basque language have in the current Basque Country for today's Basque ears? What part does pleasure in the language play bearing in mind today's young people's language experience and level? And what patience do we have as listeners, what listening abilities, to enjoy bertsos or stories on their own, even if they don't really go anywhere?

Within bertsos—in the context of language, content, form, and background—the balance is changing. Society has changed: not only strategies and methods of creation, but also the way we listen, the tempo of the sessions, and people's tastes and interests. The way of saying things has changed in bertsolaritza. Perhaps now language depends more on its essence than on enjoying it for its own sake. It is a distinction between the inside and the outside of a bertso.

"Dough made with the best flour is not bread until baked in the oven," said Xalbador.[14] Whatever the changes, we should not avoid saying that language is one of bertsos' raw materials. Bertsos lie in the poetic turns of the language (otherwise they would amount to little), and that language does have something to say. An idea. The inside and the outside, the texture and the shape, are both the essence of bertsos, both part of the message, both one.

Those insides and outsides don't necessarily always have to be the same. So, rather than the balance having changed, it would be more accurate to say that language, references,

14 Xalbador. *Odolaren mintzoa.*

the tempo of society, topics, tastes, and the way we listen, is constantly in collaborative motion.

Eyes and Ears

During change, something is always lost, and something always gained.

Today's bertsolaritza, like the world, is made more for the eye than it is for the ear. We belong to the culture of the eye, the audiovisual age, and we also learn oral improvisation by reading and writing. We live in today's fast-paced show world, and perform an activity that is oral, simple, and slow. Against all odds, successfully.

Bertsolaritza has survived because it has changed, it is constantly changing. Even so, new situations always invoke old reactions.

There has been a debate lately about standard Basque versus its dialects, "oral" versus "written" bertsolaritza. Bertsolari Igor Elortza said, "It hurts me a lot to hear that bertso language is oral for some people and literary for others."[15] Standard Basque = written = artificial, the judgement goes, and dialect = oral = natural.

Andu Lertxundi wrote that the language—Standard Basque—is not without expressiveness. "If it becomes so, it is the speaker who is incompetent."

Of course, the language has changed and evolved. As has the listener.

But even now, bertsos can provide enjoyment to and shake up listeners' ears, eyes, and brains. And today's bertsolaris master their language and work on ideas. Orally, while singing, spontaneously.

In terms of types of language and narration, each bertsolari has their own aesthetic and ideological offerings. But, as some people's bertso language is oral and others' is literary, it is hard to say whether even the most oral is actually so—because the bertsolari learned though writing. Another issue is whether to be

15 Igor Elortza, *Bertsoa.eus*, interview. August 2, 2018.

more traditional in style, with more contractions and intonation, or to deliver in dialect.

Clowns use their noses, magicians their jokes // and bertsolaris have their own language.[16] What is the "natural" way of speaking today? What is considered "oral" today?

All of a sudden, every bertsolari is taught at bertso school? Homo erectus, rising from paper to improvisation …

Orality

What is orality today?

There is no orality. No pure orality. When some people say orality, they mean uncontaminated, pure orality, and supposedly "real" orality. In other words, orality is broader than ever. It can stem from many sources. Not just from "coming up with it."

Coming up with bertsos and mastering oral improvisation is learned through writing, then performing it orally.

Today in the Basque Country, everyone has written culture; we have all grown up in an audio-visual environment; we are all influenced by music and many have studied it. All of this makes us who we are, and inevitably affects our orality.

In fact, orality is said to be most common in writing. WhatsApp messages, for example, are written in oral format: written orality.

Nowadays, what we give orally is also influenced by the written, visual, and audio cultures (among others). In theatre and cinema, creations arise first in writing. Writing in order to speak. You learn to form spontaneous bertsos through writing. Verbally spectacular things are recounted. People watch bertsos. Bertsolaris can "read" rhymes in their heads. A kind of synaesthesia.

What, then, is orality today?

What is performed orally?

Audio, written, and audiovisual sound distillation?

Air, structureless air?

Another matter would be to examine how learning through writing has affected the brain of today's bertsolaris and the

16 Agin Laburu, Gipuzkoa Championship Final, 2019. Farewell.

way in which they listen. What would have resulted had they learned otherwise?[17] We might have heard rhymes differently in our heads, for example, or felt differently about them, or came up with different combinations, had we not read them with our eyes beforehand.

Creative stimulus, a means of unlearning, another aesthetic choice. Maybe it would bring us that fresh breeze that we feel from time to time when we hear something put together in a new, unfamiliar way (rap, for example). A strange rhyming combination created by someone who has learned beyond the rules.

Today, rhyming words often share a written form, rather than a sound.[18] Rhyme for the eye rather than for the ear.

Bertso Schools: On the Way to Becoming Conservatories?

Theories about the activity of bertsolaritza (Egaña, Sarasua, Garzia, Bertsozale Association) have led to a more precise, analytical, and self-critical attitude about what we, as bertsolaris, do.

The more theorized development of bertsolaris by the younger generation, combined with the championships and their growing demands, have led to bertsolaris practicing their bertsos far more. Written work, studiously prepared work, more elaborate work. This has brought bertsolaritza to an all-time high.

The level of bertso, and its impact on society, is also the highest it has ever been. The same is true for the study materials and bertso schools' methodical approach. There are many sessions, sometimes ostentatious ones. And there are means and networks to get it out into society: television, webpages, and bertso schools in the Basque towns, to name a few.

Unlike when we started, today the bertsolari is a well-known, acknowledged figure in Basque culture, at least to some extent. I never went through "wanting to be a bertsolari." While

17 EHBE (Euskal Herriko Bertsozale Elkartea) and teacher Mikel Artola are developing a new method of teaching bertsolaritza, based on paperless, spontaneous work from the first moment.

18 "Neurrian libre." *Pure Data*. Maialen Lujanbio.

it wasn't the highest aim for young people back then, today, for many, it is. Bertsolaritza has earned this success (and risk).

Young people begin learning by imitation. What they imitate isn't a pair of baggy trousers, it's more like a different way of dressing. The flour and water are there in the patterns at bertso schools, in what bertsolaris offer.

And patterns are necessary, but they always run the risk of becoming dogmatic and all-devouring.

Anyone who comes to the academia always runs the risk of becoming standardized. What reassures me is that bertsolaritza, like a mist, is in motion and not easily captured completely, spontaneously, because it arises in an unsuspected place and is continually being transformed. Fortunately.[19]

Obviously, I am not opposed to teaching and hard work. We, too, learned from those theoretical approaches at first. But an attitude also has to be imparted, not just the technique.

Bertsolaritza and bertso schools must keep their "anarchic" spirit. Inventing ways of working. Getting together. Singing. Enjoying ourselves. Mixing things up. Trying things out.

That passion to create and try new things that the singer Anari mentioned: "We, who didn't know how to play—no chords, no rhythm—couldn't play the songs we wanted by the artists we admired. And that led us to create from the very beginning."

Everything cannot be tied to 10/8 and 7/6. We need to develop our inner voices as well. Otherwise, we would only be developing musical virtuosity. Performers who can play, but don't know how to create. Top-notch film technicians who are experts at working with cameras and digital effects, but who don't have a solid story beyond the effects. We take extraordinary leaps at bertso schools, where the students are incredibly skilful at the 10/8 construction, and repeat rhyme lists to the millimetre, but who don't have much to say.

Bertso in a conservatory setting wouldn't work. Bertso school was, is, and should be, a workshop, a meeting place.

19 "ARIAL 12, lerroartea 1'5, marjinak 2'5cm." Opening session of the Basque Country University Summer Courses. Maialen Lujanbio.

Meetings, demonstrations, anarchy, work, laughter, disorder … Everyone's work. Invaluable work.

Learning and unlearning.

Learning About Art and the Art of Learning

There is hardly any other place to train young people to create using words and reasoning. Nowadays bertso schools are one of the few places—if not the only—for working on the language, the aesthetics of the language, reasoning and worldview, the technique of self-expression, registers, words, and so on. One of the few sites to cultivate young people's creative thinking. "For teenagers and young people with a creative profile, this is perhaps the only place to get creative, at least in a collective context. What's more, for many people who have been involved in other cultural areas, it seems that bertsolaritza has been a greenhouse for new talent."[20]

Systematization, standardization, creating patterns. Even if there is always the risk of losing something, what is gained is far greater. This work has led to the sound health of today's bertsolaritza.

Thanks to bertso schools, bertsolaritza lives on. It is culture, not folklore. Thanks to bertso schools, there are more bertsolaris and more bertso fans than ever before. Knowledge about bertsolaritza is the most widespread it has ever been. Thanks to bertso schools, women have immersed themselves in bertsolaritza and claimed their place. Thanks to bertso schools, bertsolaritza has a similar organized network from town to town in all senses, from the artistic to the logistic. Thanks to bertso schools and the individual work carried out by bertsolaris, bertsolaritza is now at its highest level. Non-regulated bertso schools enable weekly meetings for adults and young people to enjoy bertsos simply and purely. It is not productive, it is not copyrighted, it doesn't require investment; it's purely enjoyment.

20 Zubiri and Aierdi Urraza, *Kultura ez da bat-batekoa.*

It is true that regulating the method can lead to standardization and a loss of nuances, but the point is what is gained and what is lost.

...and to learn the rules, so they can be broken.

References

Iriondo, Joxemari, and Antton Haranburu. "Bertsolaritza gaur eta bihar." *Jakin*, no. 14–15 (1980): 38–49.

Lujanbio, Maialen. "As the Tree Grows, the Bark Cracks." In *Female Improvisational Poets: Challenges and Achievements in the Twentieth Century*, edited by Xabier Irujo and Iñaki Arrieta Baro. Center for Basque Studies, University of Nevada, Reno, 2019.

Zubiri, Harkaitz, Retortillo, Alfredo, and Xabier Aierdi Urraza. *Kultura ez da bat-batekoa: bertsolaritza aztergai*. Bilbao: Universidad del País Vasco/Euskal Herriko Unibertsitatea, 2019.

Improvisation and Life: The *Oholtza* Project as an Example of New Artistic Proposals for *Bertsolaris*

Beñat Romera del Cerro
Artistic name: Beñat Krolem

Beñat graduated cum laude with a degree in fine arts from the University of the Basque Country in 2013, after studying a year at the University of the West of England, Bristol. He continued his training by studying filming, video, and TV. From 2015 to 2016 he combined his artistic work with a master's degree in painting at the University of the Basque Country and in La Taller (engraving workshop in Bilbao), where he was also a workshop and gallery assistant. He has received different creation grants, such as the Antonio Gala Foundation Grant in 2014, as well as the Mintzola Ahozko Lantegia, and Mikel Laboa Katedra Research Grant in 2015, among others. In 2016 he was awarded a scholarship by the Basque Government for the completion of his doctoral thesis. Today he works as a Ph.D. researcher. His line of doctoral and artistic research focuses on improvisation in art.

Abstract

The bertso-eskolak (improvisational poetry schools) have been indispensable in the stewardship of oral improvisation education and have ensured the survival and development of its practice. Within a constantly evolving landscape, how should we operate in regard to the pedagogy of bertsolaritza (improvisational poetry practice)? And more importantly, what does the practicing artist investigate? "For each new cultural time, in art a new operating type of existential sensibility is created" (Oteiza, 2013). In this way, the bertsolariak (improvisational poets), from their unique creative perspectives, are constantly creating new operating types through their experimentation. For that reason, the bertso-eskolak must be a bridge between the personal creative laboratories of the bertsolari, and life, and they must also be open to transformation as well as being agents for transformation. The challenge of new educational proposals must be constantly tackled, precisely because improvisation has the capacity to renew and change what is known. In this chapter, I will suggest new artistic proposals for the contemporary education of bertsogintza.

Translator's notes:

* Exclusively for ease of reading, the English version opts to use the pronoun/possessive *he/his* throughout the text.

** *Oholtza* literally translates as platform or stage, but after consultation with the author of this article, we have concluded that in this text he uses this term to imply "play space."

The Everyday

When studying improvisation, the first thing to remember is that improvisation's natural habitat is everyday life. Improvisation is not an activity separated from the experience of life, nor is it an elitist act, but rather the opposite; it is a continuous part of the activity of everyday life, of the experience of life. It is therefore an intrinsic feature of the human being. The need to take immediate decisions throughout the whole experience of living means our very existence forces us to improvise. Before entering into art, an artist is part of life, because the artist comes from life. Jorge Oteiza made us aware of two different revolutionary behaviors of artists:

> Before, inside the art laboratory; and after, in life. Life enters the artist's laboratory, but until the artist finishes, the work of art remains unresolved and meaningless to others. Unless the artist embellishes, but the artist is

unnecessary if he embellishes. A work of art does not educate; it is an experimental tool.[1]

An artist is most at home when experimenting. Through the practice of their craft the artist reveals our surroundings, and it is via the artist's journey that the meaning and significance of what surrounds us all, namely everyday life, becomes visible.

In an interview conducted by Josep Lluís Galiana with musician and sound artist Wade Matthews, there is a very perceptive passage on the relationship between everyday life and art:

> I believe that there is a moment when science wants to convince us that there is no longer any magic, that magic is nothing more than superstition. So the artist takes on the role of proving that there is magic and begins to highlight the magic of the everyday. It is the time when the pedestals of sculptures begin to disappear. When the pedestal, whose function was fundamentally to isolate, like the frame of a painting, begins to disappear, because it is no longer understood, as it was when works of art were produced in the nineteenth century, as something that occupies a space outside the everyday, as if the aesthetic and artistic experience were the experience of something outside the everyday. Precisely when pedestals begin to disappear, art starts to be understood as part of the everyday. Sculptures stand directly on the ground just like us, and what art can do is open up the magic of the everyday to us.[2]

The magic that Wade Matthews refers to is the mystery that drives our relationship with art and artistic practice as a species. It is an act of pure discovery in which, when we witness the act of creation, we consequently see through the eyes of

1 Oteiza, Jorge. *Ley de los cambios. Alzuza* (Navarre): Fundación Museo Oteiza Fundazio Museoa, 2013, p.12.
2 Galiana, Josep Lluís. *Improvisación libre. El gran juego de la deriva sonora.* Valencia: EdictOràlia Llibres i Publicacions, 2019, p. 150.

the creator. The painter Juan Uslé used to reminisce about the spontaneous creation of his father's drawings in his childhood:

> Another fantastic moment, and also a kind of contact with the magic of drawing and lines, was the discovery that with a single movement you can represent the world. And that discovery was precisely through my father. I remember many wintry moments. There was no heating then . . . we would be around the fire with brown paper from the packages or wrappings that they bought from him or brought from the city for the nuns, my father with a wooden stick or a piece of firewood struggling, but in a very mature, flowing way, drawing different types of birds . . . that seemed like magic to us.[3]

The relationship between an artist and his* drawing is shaped in unison, just as fire finds its dance. Thanks to the altered art object, the artist is transformed. It is precisely this capacity to project the drawing that amazes us and is what Juan Uslé is dazzled by. He refers to the experience around the fire, the embers, the stark material, where the sudden drawings project the imagination of both author and observer. John Berger also reflects on drawing and its ability to project: "A line, an area of tone, is not really important because it records what one has seen, but because of what it will lead you on to seeing."[4] His text emphasizes that discovery is a part of learning, a fragile revelation whose redemptive power rips open.

There is liberation in leaving everything behind: of relying initially on support to subsequently cast off what is known, tear down some of the supporting pillars, question them, correct them, enlarge them, cut them, and prune them with precision. But let us not forget the spiritual rhythm surrounding creation.

3 Video excerpt of an interview with the painter Juan Uslé from minute 13:44 to 14:36. Retrieved from: https://www.rtve.es/alacarta/videos/talento-100/talento-100-capitulo-1/1538804/.

4 Berger, John. *Sobre el dibujo*. Barcelona: Editorial Gustavo Gili, 2011, p.7. Translator's note: author quotes Spanish translation/publication but quote in English version is taken from original.

The Japanese, a people sensitive and open to the everyday, call this *myō* (miao). In Zen, the true artist is the one who knows how to appreciate the *myō* of things. In Zen terms, the most supreme or elevated moment of the artist's fluidity is when they experience *satori*. Daisetz T. Suzuki writes the following about *satori*:

> To experience *satori* is to become conscious of the Unconscious (*mushin*, no-mind), psychologically speaking. Art has always something of the Unconscious about it. The *satori* experience, therefore, cannot be attained by the ordinary means of teaching or learning. It has its own technique in pointing to the presence in us of a mystery that is beyond intellectual analysis. Life is indeed full of mysteries, and wherever there is a feeling of the mysterious, we can say there is Zen in one sense or another.[5]

For this reason an improviser's greatest strength is their link with everyday life; it feeds the improviser with problems, material, and possibilities. Everyday life is full of interactions that feed into an improviser's resources and assist him in putting those resources to good use; hence interaction is one of the main drivers of improvisation. Interaction, as the word suggests, is reciprocal between two or more objects, people, questions, ideas, agents, or elements. It constitutes one of the most important parts of the improvisation process and refers to the action of analyzing and linking. We have to immediately deal with information received at a precise moment by our senses. This requires the improviser to adapt their way of filtering the information they already store in their memory and that which they pick up at that precise moment to the needs of interaction with the place and the people, in a specific context. Gonzalo Abril claims:

---

5 Suzuki, Daisetz T. *El zen y la cultura japonesa*. Barcelona: Paidós, 2014, p.149. Translator's note: author quotes Spanish translation/publication but quote in English version is taken from original.

> Improvisation practice forms part of everyday activity and experience, even when, as also happens in the context of artistic improvisation, the improvisation consists of adjusting one's behavior to the requirements of interaction with others, to reciprocation in the context of life, to the continuous construction of rationality and order required by the need to give meaning and continuity to our experience.[6]

To be an improviser the essential requirements are: interaction, the ability to observe using one's senses, and constant method modification. The uniqueness of everyday life should also be mentioned as a defining element because that is precisely what shapes our attitude, and thanks to this we are able to expand our openness and way of reacting.

In an interview with historian and professor Juan Carlos Romera Nielfa,[7] we are made aware of the everyday nature and inertia of routine, as well as the diversity and singularity of the everyday.

> The everyday is, above all, a chronological axis that articulates what is repeated, but also what is exceptional and extraordinary. Therefore, what is special and unique is not an external space to the everyday. In turn, the everyday of today conditions the everyday of the future, so that repeated elements and unique events shape the living articulations of what we will later interpret as everyday. Thus, the relationship between the experience and the accumulated memory of previous experiences makes each individual's everyday unique. What is everyday for one person will not be everyday for another.[8]

6 Preface by Gonzalo Abril in Alonso, Chefa. *Improvisación libre la composición en movimiento*. Pontevedra: Dos Acordes, 2008, p.9.

7 Juan Carlos Romera Nielfa, doctor of geography and history, and qualified teacher. He has taught in primary and secondary schools. He currently lectures in the School of Education at the University of the Basque Country, Bilbao.

8 Romera Nielfa, Juan Carlos, interview by Beñat Romera del Cerro, in-person interview conducted at his house in Bilbao, October 16, 2020.

Romera Nielfa insists that the everyday is not synonymous with ordinariness and closely ties the repetitive everyday and the extraordinary everyday, since mystery is a momentum that starts in the everyday.

As a species, we do not see and understand the world in an isolated, separate, or contained way, but rather we see objects, phenomena as a whole that develop and change with their own circumstances and context. The ability to link is key to developing an artistic gaze. In the case of the improviser, he needs to improve his vision of associations in a short space of time and take them to a higher, more complex, and effective plane. He must be swift in the analysis of the information he receives at a precise moment and place, but must also link this information to what he already knows, to his personal background. It is this process that makes human thought interesting, not only as a generator of ideas, but also as a way of relating things.

The improviser already knows that the way he develops his network of connections is a process that will be shared with the audience. Both in sound and visual improvisation, the improviser agrees to let the audience in on an open and consequently transparent process. That is why the uncontrollable, irrepressible nature of life provides the ideal conditions for improvisation—precisely because both life and improvisation share the same qualities. They are real-time activities, where performance and the experience of experiencing are inseparable. Life is to improvisation what improvisation is to life, or in other words, life is improvisation because improvisation is life. Emilio Lledó wrote, "The world of what is real is sustained by the beat of a single day. It is that immediacy of each moment . . . that shapes the meaning of life."[9]

9 Introductory sentence by Emilio Lledó in "Anexo a la tercera edición." Galiana, Josep Lluís. *Improvisación libre. El gran juego de la deriva sonora*. Valencia: EdictOràlia Llibres i Publicacions, 2019, p. 221.

The Drift of Conversation: *Harria*, *Belea* and *Belakia*[10]

Improvisation can be seen in all areas of life and is part of the human condition. It is an anthropological ethos innate to us because of the very condition of living. Although animals also display improvisation-related skills, in no way do theirs resemble the skills of human beings. It is the complex way that ideas are elaborated, interrelated, and coupled with deep structure that allows them to project with, for, toward, and in an instant. Improvisation always abides by certain structures, conditions, laws, or limits that are "enablers" of the task of improvisation. By learning these limits it is possible to take a calculated risk and stay alert when creating. To improvise, you need a foundational structure upon which to smoothly build your improvisation. This structure might be a specific atmosphere, a technique, an object, a basic law, or ourselves. Although the type of structure varies, foundations are essential to support freedom of action. The dancer Steve Paxton wrote about this matter:

> To do two shows with a process of no process, would they end up being different performances? But having worked on Contact Improvisation to see if I could figure out why this thing called improvisation has a reputation for not having structure, I kept finding structure. At a certain point I decided that the structure was me. That I couldn't get outside of that. I couldn't continue the process because I kept running into myself.[11]

Ordinary speech illustrates how everyday improvisation truly is. We use words and string them together from our relationship with other speakers. We form sentences from vocabulary learned and grammar that provides constructive conditions. It is thanks to this common pre-established order

10 *Harria*: stone. *Belea*: crow. *Belakia*: sponge.
11 Paxton, Steve. Excerpt taken from "Steve Paxton, Drafting Interior Techniques" exhibition dossier in Azkuna Zentroa Alhóndiga Bilbao: Culturgest, February 20–May 10, 2020 (postponed by the Covid 19 pandemic and subsequently extended), p.23.

that we can improvise what we are going to say, what we want to express. In this sense, Stephen Nachmanovitch's explanation is relevant when he states:

> When we think improvisation, we tend to think first of improvised music or theater or dance; but beyond their own delights, such art forms are doors into an experience that constitutes the whole of everyday life. We are all improvisers. The most common form of improvisation is ordinary speech. As we talk and listen, we are drawing on a set of building blocks (vocabulary) and rules for combining them (grammar). These have been given to us by our culture. But the sentences we make with them may never have been said before and may never be said again. Every conversation is a form of jazz. The activity of instantaneous creation is as ordinary to us as breathing.[12]

Our bodies and conversation are two of the most ordinary and common forms of improvisation. Even when writing this article, I proposed open conversations to several people working in different fields, a kind of drifting dialogue where, by contrast or by proximity, the ideas and connections of conversation participants would guide the dialogue's direction. I used flâneur-like conversations to obtain answers or gain knowledge about improvisation; in short, I aimed to use verbal improvisation to obtain answers precisely about verbal improvisation. Sometimes in the most common, ordinary, and daily ways or places, we find the most suitable answers.

José Miguel Martínez Sánchez,[13] professor of creative writing, is actually engaged in two parallel activities when he teaches writing: "Creative plagiarism, or the way in which an artist creatively follows a tradition (i.e. by copying someone else), and limitation, because necessity is also the mother of creativity!" To

12 Nachmanovitch, Stephen. *Free play. Improvisation in life and art.* New York: Tarcher Penguin, 1990, p. 17.

13 PhD student at the Universidad Nacional de Educación a Distancia (UNED) and professor of creative writing

explain what he means, José Miguel told me a European folk story[14] (told from Portugal to Scandinavia) to summarize these two apparently antagonistic ideas. The story is entitled "Stone Soup" and is about a group of travellers who arrive in a village in the middle of a famine carrying nothing but an empty pot. In the middle of the main square they begin to fill the pot with water and drop a large clean stone in it. One of the villagers, his curiosity piqued, approaches and asks: What are you doing? To which the travellers reply that they are preparing a delicious stone soup. The surprised villager replies that some vegetables are lacking and goes to his garden to bring what little he has and adds them to the pot. Thanks to the cooking smell, more villagers come, each one bringing what they have: spices, condiments, etc. After removing the (inedible) stone, this large pot of soup is shared by villagers and travellers alike. It is a story that brings together the two schools: tradition and limitation. The stone represents a catalyst between tradition and constant novelty. Tradition, or creative plagiarism, is a means of learning in which artists imbibe each other's work to practice other visions and ways of doing things. It is the importance of creation based on the observation of the other. It is because of creative plagiarism that tradition can persist over time, but always drawn from change—change that takes place through cooperation with another, or others, through group interaction.

Bertsolari

When developing an approach to improvisation, interaction and cooperation are important learning-exploring methods. The bertsogintza[15] Andoni Egaña refers to how there are two sides to his approach to exploring the art of improvised

14 Martínez Sánchez, José Miguel, interview by Beñat Romera del Cerro, phone interview, October 13-15, 2020.

15 In the words of the bertsolari Andoni Egaña: "A bertsolari is a person who expresses through song his ideas and thoughts in front of an audience. We are often a character, a role we play because that is what the person who launches the song requires of us.�

bertsogintza.[16]He uses the Basque words *bele* (crow) and *belaki* (sponge) to describe these two sides. By using these metaphors, he is weighing up the skills and characteristics of the bertsolari. The "thieving crow" is a bird that steals or takes food from the carelessness of others. This personification suggests that the artist takes elements, ways of doing things, words, and even interests from other people. With sponge, *belakia*, he is referring to absolute sense-based observation, a kind of attention where the bertsolari uses constant alertness to refine his craft.[17] Bertsolaris are like sponges, absorbing all they can from opportunities, and their memory and imagination are their greatest allies. For the improviser, to postpone is to resign; once the opportunity has been lost it cannot be recovered.

Today, in a global society governed mainly by immediacy and imminent *over-information*, the bertsolari, as an improviser-thinker, has remained on a different shore. His understanding of the concepts of *immediate*, *imminent*, and *present* follows altogether different criteria. For bertsolaris, improvisation is the end result of a vital process of incubation, compilation, harvesting, and artistic maturation, to later create in the moment and with the moment. A bertsolari works for/to the moment and in/from the moment. His is the art of time and presence (space-time), a performance that is limited by an indefinite duration (it is for and against time) but actually is marked by the minute hand of the vertigo of silence. It is the silence of the awaiting listeners that drives him on; the deafening moment of audience contemplation whilst they await a bertso that forces him to leap into song. The brief mystery of the silence of the wait is what gives strength to the bertsolari's song: his time of thought, the

16 A *bertso* is not a line of a stanza, but the entire verse. *Bertsogintza*, or the creation of *bertsoak* (bertsos), is an improvised, extemporaneous oral art form, delivered in the Basque language and found in the Basque Country. Although there are also so-called *bertso-paperak* (bertsoak created with a longer attention span, or bertsoak previously memorized), the status of a bertsolari, today, is gained by his skill at singing extemporaneous, improvised bertsoak. To do this, a bertsolari uses tune, meter, and rhyme, all without the aid of any instrument. Bertsolaris sing a cappella, this being one of the main differences with other oral improvisers from other cultures.

17 Extract from an interview with Andoni Egaña in Altuna, Asier. *Bertsolari*. Txintxerpe (Gipuzkoa): Txintxua films, 2011, 1:06:44.

contemplation of his creative process, and the wait for the song itself. Accompanied solitude.

During the bertsolari's performance, we find what I call the *sculpting of the bertsolari's thoughts*, in other words, the power or physical shape of the bertso thought, visually embodied by the bertsolari. This is similar to other oral arts such as flamenco with its embodiment of the cry of intonation and the lament or *grito jondo*. Each gesture and movement is part of the cry, a lament, when the flamenco singer merges into his expression, embodies it, and gives birth to the song. The sculptor, like the bertsolari or the flamenco singer, sculpts, shapes, envisions. The artist and researcher David Pavo Cuadrado says:

> Like the phlegmatic flamenco singer, the sculptor enters the sculpture: rinsing his hands, tuning them to the desire to get hold of his object, acknowledging it. This initial phase, far from being a preparation for the performance, is part of the creative process itself, and can be considered the equivalent of the cry of intonation in flamenco singing.[18]

We could say that the bertsolari is a vacuum modeller. He shapes small connections and then leaps to another, activating everything he leaves unsaid.[19] It is the leap from each vacuum that unites the listener. The anthropologist Joseba Zulaika noted this when he explained that "what the bertsolari says is just as important as what he does not say." He has the ability to frame the bertso as a negative and shape it for each listener. It is his apparent structural austerity that strikes the listener. The verse reveals itself as a tricky puzzle which, despite the idiosyncrasies and details of each bertso and

18 Pavo Cuadrado, David, quoted in Romera del Cerro, Beñat (artistic pseudonym: Krolem, Beñat). "La improvisación en bertsogintza desde el proyecto Oholtza / The improvisation in bertsogintza: the case of Oholtza project." Recovered from: http://www.lasiaweb.com/wp-content/uploads/2018/05/Comunicaciones_2018.pdf

19 Extract from an interview with Joseba Zulaika in Altuna, Asier. *Bertsolari*. Txintxerpe (Gipuzkoa): Txintxua films, 2011, 07:53.

each bertsolari, comes out in an ordered fashion—as a chain of ideas, parts, pebbles; created as images and sensations.

We could perhaps imagine a bertsolari as someone who has a kind of "shed" inside him: a place to both shelter and store things, the place where he consciously (because, of course, he practices and studies, carries out field work, has notebooks, exercises, and goes to bertso-eskolak) and unconsciously tucks away a whole repertoire of words, images, sensations, stories, readings, ideas, arguments, and sounds. Like any other creator, he plucks things from his store to create. I believe there are two unmistakable features to the bertsolari's complex technique of word sculpting: the apparent sobriety and simplicity of the bertso (not being able to say much because everything must be limited to the space of the bertso) and the final hammerblow at the end (the end of the bertso is an explosion of all the artistic discourse surrounding and performed during the bertso). A key structure of the bertso is precisely the end as a beginning; in other words, the first thing the bertsolari usually thinks about is the end of the bertso. He carves out a path, a montage of ideas all aimed at his finale, which he knows, but the audience does not. In terms of transmission and communication, this is a very powerful technique, since it achieves even greater attention and expectation from the audience. The final outcome leans on, is propped up by, tied to, slips on, and bumps into whatever comes before. The end is indeed the beginning.

Play, Not Game

In artistic practice, *play* is linked to the way the artist explores, whereas a *game* has rules and a limited outcome that is evident from its structural skeleton. In artistic research, and especially in free improvisation, play is necessary. Thanks to play, there is an open and unlimited playing field where every result is allowed. Play never ends, because the very purpose of play is play itself. The world is constantly at play. We are continually doing and trying, immersed in an insatiable search. If we are to offer quality teaching at bertso-eskolak, we must take into account play, experimentation from everyday life, and interaction. Risk-taking in the shape of play is necessary for there to be transformation, a vital quality of this oral art. We must therefore use flexible artistic practice to alter and transform the bertso-eskolak on a daily basis. Stephen Nachmanovitch writes:

> Without play, learning and evolution are impossible. Play is the taproot from which original art springs; it is the raw stuff that the artist channels and organizes with all his learning and technique. Technique itself springs from play, because we can acquire technique only by the practice of practice, by persistently experimenting and playing with our tools and testing their limits and resistances.[20]

The study of bertsogintza (bertso-crafting) at a bertso-eskola is not an end in itself, but enables the development of the bertsolari, of the person, something that is achieved through free play and experimentaion. The bertsolari is shaped by the bertso he sings. The possibility of free singing will help discern his instinct and sharpen his observation as he travels along his own developmental path. The gradual, daily consolidation of the bertso-eskola group will help collectively shape the way in which its members see, feel, and share the world. Jean-León Pallandre organized an improvisation course for children using electroacoustic media at the GMEA in Albi, France. At the conclusion, the electroacoustic pieces composed during the course were presented and two children started to discuss improvisation in tune with the pieces. One child accused the other of " -Just doing any old thing! To which the other replied -Yes, but not any old how!"[21] This anecdote sheds a lot of light on the question of judgment in improvisation and on the uniqueness of each person's everyday life and process or method. The site-specific opportunities that one child chose were not those that the other

20 Nachmanovitch, Stephen. *Free play improvisation in life and art.* New York: Tarcher Penguin, 1990, p. 42.

21 Matthews, Wade. *Improvisando. La libre creación musical.* Madrid: Turner Música publications, 2012, p. 151.

child would have chosen; in other words, the mistakes he chose as an opportunity were not the same as those of the other child.

Children's ability to improvise is clear. Many researchers concede that a person's youth greatly influences the enthusiasm with which they approach improvisation. Albert Kaul wrote:

> There is no doubt that children love to improvise. Anyone who has worked with children knows how easy it is to get them motivated; they're simply used to playing and putting all of their effort into tasks that involve, among other things, improvising. What's more, if improvisation is used to get a game started, children will usually dive head first into the improvisational activity and come up with new tasks effortlessly.[22]

An atmosphere of play is essential when teaching improvisation; every result should be welcomed. Romera Nielfa states: "Teaching is not a matter of dumping a heavy burden on the body or soul of a child; on the contrary, teaching is liberating in the sense that it has to be free and flexible... the child exerts himself, not to bear a heavy burden, but to strive for discovery."[23]

Discovery is only possible by distancing ourselves from the already known, from the obvious, from our comfort zone. There is no other way to discover than to exchange that comfort for a swampy terrain, where every step can put our whole body out of kilter as it attempts to hold on to what has already been discovered and at the same time seek to alter its familiar method. Distancing ourselves from what is known entails risk and a degree of (unclearly defined) intentionality. The blurring allows us to make fresh artistic decisions. Doing this is similar to when a painter squints at what he is looking at, precisely to see the painting more clearly, to have a better view of the path

---

22 Kaul, Albert. "The world is a game! Improvising with children." In Alonso, Chefa. *Enseñanza y aprendizaje de la improvisación libre. Propuestas y reflexiones*. (Teaching and Learning free improvisation. Ideas and reflections). Madrid: Editorial Alpuerto, 2013, p. 171.

23 Romera Nielfa, Juan Carlos, interview by Beñat Romera del Cerro, in-person interview conducted at his house in Bilbao, October 16, 2020.

towards what he is seeking: that which is not painted but is impregnated in the paint. The painter squints when pursuing what he can sense, what he can glimpse in his mind's eye. In short, he blurs things in order to see more clearly.

It is the attempts, the leaps into the void, that make learning in artistic research possible. But a leap should not be understood as random, aimless investigation since artistic practice must come to an end. When writing about the importance of conclusion in art, Jorge Oteiza refers to Demosthenes.[24] Demosthenes, a Greek orator and politician, would retire to the beach alone where he would put a few pebbles in his mouth and speak, not trying to say anything, but learning to speak. When he then spoke in public without the pebbles, he had already travelled the pedagogical path of paved soliloquies. "Today artists still have those pebbles in their mouths, having lost the sense, the taste, and the awareness, of a long, dramatic learning process that they do not know how to justify or conclude."[25] Each repetition, unique in its own right, assists us in learning to improvise. In a conversation with the artist Fernando de Uña, he explained to me: "I have realized that constant learning from a referent, even repetitive copying often makes you reject precisely that model, and move on to something else, to another matter. And that is how you assimilate the great masters and how you can assimilate your own environment."[26] The improviser guzzles down attempts, imagination, and proposals in his thirst for time. Inmaculada Jimenez explains:

> There is suspended time, outside reality, which is the time it takes for the drawing to be made. This may happen in just one session, lasting from several minutes to a few hours. And then, that's it. Although this ending does not necessarily mean that the drawing has emerged.

24 Demosthenes (Athens, 364 B.C.–Calauria, 322 B.C.): an eloquent orator and politician from Greece.
25 Oteiza, Jorge. *Ley de los cambios*. Alzuza (Navarre): Fundación Museo Oteiza Fundazio Museoa, 2013, p. 11.
26 De Uña, Fernando, interview by Beñat Romera del Cerro, phone interview, October 16, 2020.

> There are times when you have to return to it, repeat, and start again, because it's still holding out. (. . .) Each person has his or her own personal ritual with drawing, with art. It's a way of getting yourself in a position to work. But a drawing may also emerge from a group.[27]

To learn bertsogintza (the craft of the bertsolari), we need bertso-eskolak (bertso schools). These become places where risks can be taken in a much more experimental way. Romera Nielfa says:

> I am in favor of both things, focusing on the basics of art as well as encouraging everything that arises from that. (. . .) Even letting oneself get lost in experimentation, in improvisation, and always, always, nurturing one's gaze. Miró used to say that the best teacher he had was the one who summoned his students at seven in the morning to watch the sunrise. The sensation of the light of daybreak was a sensorial, plastic, artistic sensation and from that gaze of the sunset or the sunrise, even accessing different senses beyond sight, for example; smell or touch . . . the textures . . . from that vital experience with the elements, with the landscape, from them a gaze is born that can be artistic, poetic or philosophical.[28]

The crucial thing in teaching improvisation is to keep searching and exploring. Chefa Alonso explains:

> In order to be a good improviser, you need to have something to say and a personal language with which to say it. In addition to knowing how to listen and how to give space to others, you should be curious and willing to explore constantly. Good improvisers never

27 Jiménez, Inmaculada. "Los límites del dibujo y una poética de grupo," in Vélez Cea, Manuel. *El dibujo del fin de milenio*. Granada: University of Granada, 2001, p.130.

28 Romera Nielfa, Juan Carlos, interview by Beñat Romera del Cerro, in-person interview conducted at his house in Bilbao, October 16, 2020.

> feel that they have reached their goal; it's always just out of reach.[29]

Oholtza, Contemporary Exercises for a New Bertsolari

Ultimately there is no such thing as purity, but rather constant fusion and blending. Improvisation is a field of experimentation where change is a constant of daily life, where blending is a reality, and adaptability and resistance are strengths. *Oholtza* project is a contemporary art research project to transform and experiment with bertsolaris and their technique. The Basque word *oholtza* translates as platform/stage/play space,** and the Oholtza project is a process of searching that uses art research to work on new experimental parameters in improvisation as it relates to bertsolaris. In 2014, I began my first experiments with oral improvisers, mainly focusing on art with bertsolaris from all over the Basque Country, although in the *Europa bat-batean, kantu inprobisatuaren nazioarteko topaketa 2016* meeting, I also worked with *glosadors* and *repentistas*, oral improvisers from other cultures. Oholtza is a performance in which one, two, or more bertsolaris (oral improvisers) work together with me, a visual improviser. It is a project that uses constructive, movable, and hinged objects to provide a place of action for the improviser (the bertsolari in this case). It is a double game of improvisation, where the oral and the visual share time and space.

The visual piece is made of wood, metal, fabric, and LED lighting, all of which can be interconnected. Thanks to this interconnecting system, individual parts are stacked or latched together to create a sculpture or piece of architecture. This gives the performance a broader range of possibilities and variations, allowing a whole variety of compositions. I improvise by using these different objects to build a specific sculptural/architectural entity at a given time and in a given space, where creation and exhibition occur simultaneously—exactly like when a bertsolari

29 Alonso, Chef. *Enseñanza y aprendizaje de la improvisación libre. Propuestas y reflexiones* / Teaching and Learning Free Improvisation. Ideas and Reflections. Madrid: Editorial Alpuerto, 2013, p. 177.

performs. Once the construction of the performative space is complete, I select and subsequently assume one or two corporal postures within the visual system. Finally, I place my body in a final posture, which I also select in the moment. At that time, the bertsolaris move to the places and adopt the positions I first set, and their work of oral creation then begins. Adding or removing objects, and changing and transforming the space and the body of the bertsolari during the performance, means the whole process can be repeated or even changed. It is a constant sculptural metamorphosis in which changes and variations occur, even in the middle of the bertso, which alter the normal course through which the bertsolari develops his technique and, consequently, also his creative process. Nothing is decided beforehand. There is no pre-defined route. The structures created by our actions are whatever possibilities are offered by the system of objects.

The Oholtza project is based on an analysis of the relationship between the creative process of the bertso and the physical attitude of the performer on the stage, in order to propose new fields of performance through the notion of sculpting the bertsolari. Important to my theoretical reflection in this are Erwin Wurm's sculptural studies in his work *One-minute sculptures*;[30] the process involved in creating *Merzbau* by Kurt Schwitters;[31] and the *tablao* (flamenco stage), which is

30 Erwin Wurm (born 1954) is an Austrian artist. In his series One Minute Sculptures he features people – anonymous participants, performers, curators, artists and even the artist himself – engaging in unconventional and sometimes physically challenging interactions with everyday objects such as clothing, buckets, balls, doorframes, bicycles and perishable goods. The resulting compositions feature unusual contortions – held for a minute – and illogical still-lives that are both humorous and provocative. Wurm began his One Minute Sculptures in 1988, and has since been continuously contributing to the encyclopaedic series in myriad locations around the world. As well as photographs, the series comprises video and performance works. Retrieved from: https://www.tate.org.uk/art/artworks/wurm-one-minute-sculptures-p82013

31 Kurt Schwitters (Kurt Hermann Eduard Karl Julius Schwitters) was a German artist who was born in Hanover, Germany. Schwitters worked in several genres and media, including dadaism, constructivism, surrealism, poetry, sound, painting, sculpture, graphic design, typography, and what came to be known as installation art. One of the most important art works and myths in modern art, the inspiration for many installation artists, and still one of the most well known and published works by Kurt Schwitters (1887–1948), is the Merzbau which in fact, no longer exists. It was destroyed in a British air raid in October 1943 in Hannover. The Merzbau comprised a total of eight rooms in his house at 5

bent through "interaction" with Israel Galván's dancing in the film *Israel Galván* (2010) by María Reggiani.[32]

After several performances and art installations, I have reflected on the consequences of the Oholtza performances and how they affect bertsolari technique. I refer to these outcomes as "approaches," because indeed they are elements that must be interwoven with the bertsolari's creative methods in the performance from beginning to end, and they also affect the audience's understanding of the bertso. These approaches are set out below.

Approach 1: Body Position

When bertsolaris take the place of the visual improviser, two things happen which I consider to be of interest.

1.1

If two places are marked, the two participating bertsolaris must each choose one of the places and adopt the posture indicated. The place they chose (the decision they make) affects the construction of the role of each bertsolari and his bertso.

1.2

In these performances, bertsolaris are not restricted to taking the position they usually do in this oral art form. (Generally a bertsolari will sit or stand in front of the audience. Although they can move, and *bertso-bazkariak*, or "experimental actions,"

Waldhausenstraße in Hanover. Most of the surviving photographs seem to have been taken in the space of the 'Merzbau proper' ('eigentlicher Merzbau'), in which Schwitters is known to have begun working at the beginning of 1927. Based on these photographs, the stage designer Peter Bissegger executed a reconstruction of the 'Merzbau proper' between 1981 and 1983, assisted and supported by the artist's son Ernst Schwitters. Harald Szeemann commissioned Bissegger to make a one-to-one reconstruction and it formed part of his famous exhibition Der Hang zum Gesamtkunstwerk, which included other reconstructions of this kind. After the exhibition tour the reconstruction was bought and permanently installed in the Sprengel Museum Hannover. Retrieved from: https://www.tate.org.uk/research/publications/tate-papers/08/kurt-schwitters-reconstructions-of-the-merzbau

32 Reggiani, Maria. Israel Galván. Madrid: Mare Films, ARTE France, Les Films d'Ici, A Negro Producciones, 2010.

are allowed, this art form is usually rather static.) Although the bertsolari does not need movement to create, in Oholtza he is forced to initiate and decide upon a movement that alters his traditional position: for example, by singing lying down or with his back to the audience. Obviously, these conditions will have consequences both to the singing (singing lying down is complicated for the vocal chords; singing with one's back to the crowd means the sound cannot travel directly to the audience) and to the performance (the audience is more directly involved with the bertsolari's body; the meaning of the message may be altered due to the physicality involved).

Approach 2: Materials

Thanks to the system of assembled parts and LEDs that can also be used as creative material, it is impossible to predict what might happen.

2.1

Unlike a subject or role that is imposed, in Oholtza the bertsolari has to use his creative freedom in his position and attitude towards his creation. Additionally, his sculptural reading of the performance (what he sees and projects from his imagination), will be affected by the response of the other bertsolari. For example, what one bertsolari understands (figuratively speaking) as a bed, might be a grave for the other bertsolari. This creates a confrontation that is gradually played out in the improvised conversation itself (both the role of each person, and what is said or how it is said, has to be molded as the performance takes shape). The standard thought process of the bertsolari ("the beginning is the end") is turned on its head because he must alter his ending, must constantly innovate, depending on these various factors.

The audience also enters into this visual triangle, because the listener not only hears but also sees, and makes a

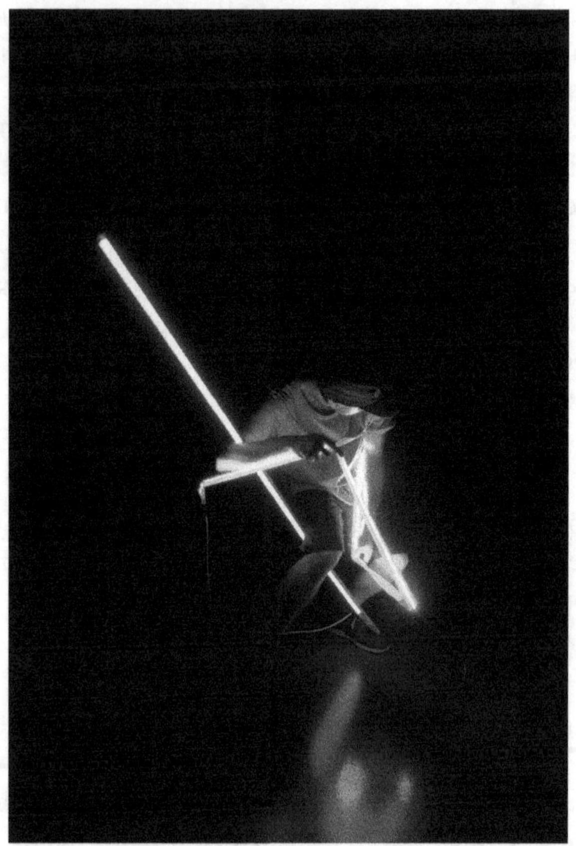

visual construction in his or her own head. One can hear the audience discussing in hushed tones: *It's like...*; *I think it's a...*; *It looks like...*; *It reminds me of...* From this moment onward, the audience begins to sculpt and enter the sculpture. In an inviting atmosphere, they participate in the common artistic experience, in the performative composition. The sculptural work engages the audience, even taking the bodies of the audience as a possibility—as sculptural material and a creative tool.

The performance also broadens the range of the audience to include those who cannot speak Basque. The meaning of the bertso is lost on these non-Basque-speakers, and is freed from forming part of the message of the perfomance. Although this kind of audience does not understand the words, they follow the

artistic piece visually and phonetically, experiencing the words in Basque as a material without linguistic meaning, drawing its phonetic-poetic power outwards.

2.2

Sometimes, as a visual improviser, I add variations right in the middle of the singing of the bertso. This forces the bertsolari to restructure and change the dynamic of his technique, and may affect the end of the bertso. His awareness is heightened, and by playing around with methodology the bertsolari's results and procedural rules of creating are changed.

Approach 3: "Mistakes"

The ideas of communication-incommunication-pre-communication[33] articulate an important part of the project, especially the way the three overlap. Art, amazingly, seems to be a pre-communicative state, since art does not only inform but goes beyond text and context. Despite this, the bertsolari is concerned about content, message, and narrative-poetic thread. The Oholtza project attempts to distance bertsolaris from mere communication and activate a kind of subversive language game, accessing what is socially known as language mistakes. Risk allows for the creation of visual stutters and broken but then (thanks to improvisation) mended bertsos. Sensitive balance is fighting for improvised creation, sometimes not fully reaching its best. This produces what academically we understand as mistakes, failures, and weaknesses, but which (far from hurting the performance) gives it its unique characteristics and enriches the improvised act.

Conclusion

The Oholtza project is branching out into performances such as *Ejercicios urbanos para un bertsolari* (Urban exercises for a bertsolari) and the *Gora potoa!* project. With the experience gained over several years in this line of research, I have created a book of performative drawings. In it, I propose different contemporary exercises for bertsolaris. The intention is to explore this oral art from other points of view and provide bertso-eskolak with additional training and teaching exercises. Imagination will determine which spaces are appropriate for Oholtza, and where the necessary risk can be taken to produce change and transformation. The unfathomable space of an idea is located between the extremes of silence and din, and after initial steps through the labyrinth of improvisation, this idea sometimes becomes a clear and direct utterance.

---

33 See: *Komunikazio-inkomunikazioa* by the artist Mikel Laboa.

A Coda

Larraitz Ariznabarreta

Larraitz Ariznabarreta (Bilbao 1968) is an assistant professor at the William A. Douglass Center for Basque Studies at the University of Nevada, Reno. Her fields of research deal with the analysis of various expressions of Basque culture and their relations with power.

Abstract

The epilogue to the book delves into the institutionalization of bertsolaritza as a contributor to its modernization, looks at the tensions that different ideological impulses in this institutionalization have created, and suggests new questions for further research.

> Canon is a loaded term these days, in more ways than one. Etymologically it ultimately derives from the same forebear as does cannon, its more transparently pyrotechnic sibling. Cannons have always exploded; now, more and more, the canon is imploding. Most tellingly for humanities curricula on the eve of the new millennium, canon has come to designate a battlefield, an intellectual fortress under siege, a primary site for cultural combat.
> (Foley, 1998, p. 13)

To discuss the history of Basque bertso schools is to examine the process of institutionalization —and ulterior canonization— of the art of improvisational singing within the (minority) realm of Basque speakers.[1] Reversely, the discussion on bertsolaritza's organizational structuring necessarily involves crediting that very accomplishment for the modern thrust and contemporary triumph of the once frumpy rural tradition among Basque (smart) urban devotees.

Every social group institutionalizes its pattern of behavior based on the common understanding of who the group is and what that identity means. One could go so far as to say that such markers make us who we are, though seldom in any evident way. According to Scott (2014, p. 56), "Institutions comprise regulative, normative and cultural-cognitive elements that, together with associated activities and resources, provide meaning and stability to social life." Henceforth, the reference to the institutionalization of bertsolaritza and the operational establishment of bertso schools is highly relevant when discussing the art's modern success, current contradictions, and future challenges.

Admittedly, the term school necessarily implies some grade of institutionalization. In the case of oral culture, this institutionalization tends to lead to the progressive formalization and fixation of the fluid and more casual happenings of impromptu performances, eventually mirroring the formerly oral styles to those of the written-driven culture products and transferring its spaces from marginal backlands to urban centers. In that sense, as unpopular as the assertion may seem, the institutionalization of orality looks a lot like an appropriation of the ancient primitive by the modern developed powers, which take it into (assimilate it to) their own culture capital.

Although most would agree that the gains compensate for the losses, the move of bertsolaritza from cider houses and village squares to the rule of (albeit informal) academia —its

1 Here, by referring to the institutionalization of bertsolaritza we are considering (i) its organizational structuring—the creation of the Association of Bertsolaris of the Basque Country (1985) [The Association changed its name in 1996 to: Euskal Herriko Bertsozale Elkartea (Association of Friends of Bertsolaritza)], (ii) its subsequent diffusion through modern media, and (iii) the proliferation of non-formal bertso schools in the seventies and its "practice in statutory education" (Garzia, Egana, & Sarasua, 2001, p. 45) in more recent years.

institutionalization and intellectualization[2]—has not been devoid of aesthetic and ideological tensions.

For one, there are still those who underscore that one of the principal failures of bertsolaritza's rise in social acceptance was the loss of its initial freshness and primal glee. This trend is apparently—if not universal—quite common worldwide throughout times and cultures. In fact, it is to be found in all kinds of folk literature, arts, or music. To mention one well-known specific case, we find such an example in the development of blues music: From—first—lonely, rural, guitar-playing black men, chanting their grievances from town to town; to—later—urban, black women, singing to growing audiences; to—eventually—black records selling well to both black and white mainstream; to—ultimately—changing the old forms of real blues to refer to either a pure form or any sad song (or thing).

The riddle-like evolution seems applicable to bertsolaritza. The very steps toward modern big-ticket success have pushed it to a similar de-oralization of its practices. To name just a few of the landmarks: from disdain to appreciation; from casual exercise to set-up performances and sports-warlike txapelketa (championship, first called bertso-gudu, or bertso battle); from Francoist darkness and resistance to shiny celebration; from rural (elderly) minority to widespread (young) audience; from events to records; and—as institutionalization progressed—from taverns to mass (and digital) media, to schools (both informal bertso schools and in statutory schooling, and eventually academia too). In a nutshell, through the instruction of larger groups and more appreciative art-minded peers, bertso schools have resulted in

2 Modern bertsolaritza has become intellectualized both in content and form: "(i) deep theorization; (ii) more comprehensive and updated global information; (iii) a trend towards analytical perspective; and (iv) emphasis on conceptual interpretation account for bertsolaritza's changes in content. Equivalently, bertsolaritza's structural formal features have followed a similar intellectualizing trend: (i) specific preparation on the part of the verse improvisers; (ii) the recourse to new literary tropes and semantic resources, which transcend traditional formulaic (popular) metaphors and unchanging cyclical view of the world; together with (iii) a proliferation of modern, more sophisticated tunes, all constitute formal characteristics of (modern) Basque improvisational verse singing." Ariznabarreta, 2019, pp. 125-126.

the main activist nuclei of that process of modernizing the old heritage of bertsolaritza.

Parallelly, the unorthodox force of a minority culture—whose followers still perceive themselves as collective feats of dissent and resistance[3]—somewhat conflicts with its close connections to the very policy makers they often oppose."[4] Indeed, one could argue that many of the characteristics defining modern bertsogintza originate in the dichotomy that arises from the eulogization by its aficionados and Basque public institutions alike.[5] While the Bertsozale Elkartea owes part of its success to the historic support of the Basque administration, many bertsolaris—whose sphere of influence is not confined to bertsolaritza—contest the homogenizing force of mass culture, and (covertly, at least) resent the various governments and authorities that hinder the full emancipation of Basque language and culture. Similarly, a close dialectical relationship has been established by the improvisers and their fandom, who, in general terms at least, are receptive of a certain shared ethos: they also perceive the Basque cultural capital as unique to their particular group and believe it constitutes a symbolic wealth that needs to be zealously protected (by policy makers) against homogenization. Therefore, whereas a certain nostalgia

3 "Arguably, the most obvious way in which bertsolaritza functions as a tool of cultural resistance is found in the linguistic situation of the region. Because Basque speakers are a minority within their own territory, speaking Euskara and practicing a form of improvisation based on this language can be viewed as a form of resistance." Mouillot, 2009, p. 7.

4 "Regarding public administration bodies, the Bertsozale Elkartea requests help from and offers help to them involving those projects deemed to be of public interest. The socio-cultural project of bertsolaritza has a significant degree of autonomy with respect to the political administration, given that the artistic activity (bertsogintza) in which it is based is quite self-sufficient economically in a modest way and so does not have to depend on public government purse-strings. Nevertheless, it is true that, regarding the pillars of the Bertsozale Elkartea (transmission, dissemination and archiving-research) there is a significant area of cooperation with the public authorities." Garzia, Egana, & Sarasua, 2001, p. 75.

5 "Bertsozale Elkartea is an association open to all types of relations both within Basque language culture (such as Basque public administration and other bodies) as well as with international organizations. It has good relations with other social groups which are involved in Basque culture, with the Basque public administration, political parties, social movements, and private bodies within Basque society as well as with artists experiences in improvised singing at an international level." Garzia, Egana, & Sarasua, 2001, p. 74.

for counterculture characterizes bertsolaris and their cohorts, "bertsolaritza (and its improvised component) cannot be grasped solely in terms of resistance." As Mouillot contends:

> The recent appearance of Basque broadcast media utilizing and contributing to the popularity of bertsolaritza (Basque television and radio stations), recordings and transcriptions of bertsos (a task mostly accomplished by the Bertsozale Elkartea documentation center), and the organization of large-scale events, are all elements pointing towards a form of mass production which certainly challenges the values of spontaneity and accessibility inherent in improvised practices. As we have seen, these tendencies appear fundamentally to be elements of a global super culture, and if they are easy to criticize (as "inauthentic" or as having the effect of leveling cultural differences) they nonetheless appear as tools of an effective process of modernization for the Basque cultural project. (Mouillot, 2009, p. 8)

In fact, not unlike many other facets of Basque culture, bertsolaritza has evolved from a defensive and ritualistic "small traditional coterie"[6] into a widely accessible post-industrial culture practice that attracts a (relatively) large number of urban youths. In that sense, Xabier Amuriza's theoretical prelude to bertso schools, the claim that anyone could be coached in the craft of improvisational singing, resonates with the dismissal of inborn-essentialists views of what constituted Basqueness in the past,[7] while it echoes the more inclusive—and institutionalized—schemata of contemporary Basque identity construal. An ideological schema which "for several decades now clearly advocates a civic, inclusive form of nationalism that is staunchly opposed to any ethnic, racial or linguistic definition of what it means to be Basque."[8]

6 Ariznabarreta, 2019, p. 10

7 "All we know is as a result of learning, the only and big difference lies in the method of learning." Xabier Amuriza cited by Mindegia, 2019.

8 Ruiz-Vieytez, 2016, p. 228.

The alluded to (radical) social turn "is also a turn in its interpretative framework which implies a metamorphosis of multiple dimensions"[9] and runs parallel to the development of the Basque collective we-ness and self-referentiality in the so-called Autonomic Era (1979–2020). As (Larrinaga & Amurrio, 2016, p. 101) contend: "Eminently political action at the macro-social level becomes action that is principally cultural, and also technical, developed in the micro-spaces of everyday life. This turn enables the confrontation to become collaboration or, in the worst of cases, a non-aggression pact with the autonomous power." Although it is challenging to determine whether the evolution of bertsolaritza merely mirrors that social change or has been, in fact, an important grip in that development, it is apparent that both processes are socially and politically connected. In fact, similar parallelisms can be drawn when analyzing the role of other educational schemes such as the Basque medium school (Ikastola) movement.

As supportive hubs of socialization—and, hence, "a meeting place to develop a wide range of personal and social skills"[10]—bertso schools have been pivotal in the alluded transformation. Albeit originally conceived as strongly politically engaged spaces that replicated the defensive stance of Basque nationalism and aimed at the transmission of an art (and a culture) that were on the verge of disappearance, the evolution of these informal educational schemes has long revealed an effort for equilibrium between the characteristics of a traditional arts academia, centers of self-expression, and social hubs in the broadest of senses. Bertso schools have now become public spaces for social—rather than political—resistance where such elements as the marginalization of Euskara, traditional gender construction, and other social norms are overtly challenged. As Oihana Iguaran, a contributor to this collection, conceded to the newspaper Berria on March 5, 2020:

9 Larrinaga & Amurrio, 2016, p. 101.
10 Oihana Iguaran, bertsolari and researcher, in: Arin & Satrustegi, 2020.

> [Bertso schools are more than] a group of friends, a network, a family. [. . .] A space to grow, a space to enjoy. In addition to technical skills, the bertso-school is also a meeting place for developing a wide range of personal and social skills. It is a space to reflect and dig into many topics; it helps to identify concerns and build a perspective to look at the world [. . .]. It is also an area for the bertsolari to develop critical thinking. [. . .] (Bertso schools are) a training in dialectics. (Arin & Satrustegi)

We agree with Iguaran when she claims that bertso schools have operated as "spaces for social transformation" and have provided Basque youths with "training in dialectics." Moreover, we believe that bertso schools serve as a meaningful metaphor of the evolution of Basque culture and society in the last four decades and provide a synthesis of its many contradictions. The two (2009, 2017) championships of Maialen Lujanbio, an attendee to their local bertso school in Hernani (Gipuzkoa) since its establishment, are expressive in the way they describe this ideological development and its dissemination:

> Those little droplets of bertsolaritza renewal became rivulets, and the rivulets, with the new generation, would become a wave. We caught the wave, or maybe the wave caught us. Young bertsolaris modernized and adapted bertsolaritza to their times. They introduced new attitudes, aesthetics, and subjects: drugs, alternative discourses about love and sexual relationships, different cultural references, different ways of singing, of using the language. (Lujanbio 2019: 88)

Whereas this volume constitutes an important step in the right direction, there are still research questions that we deem essential in the analysis of the development of bertso schools (and their group identity constituents), the institutionalization process of bertsolaritza, and the power dynamics associated with it. Do bertso school attendees share a we-ness beyond that of an acute consciousness of belonging to a minoritized culture? What are some of the ideological characteristics of that we-ness? How are the inner schemata of that collective identity represented through discourse? What are its recurrent motifs? Are there any ideological taboos involved? What is the specific contribution of the Basque Regional Government, and its provincial administrations, in the raise and rise of bertsolaritza? Does institutional support restrict the field of action (from the national to the local) of bertso schools? What are the qualitative gains and failures (if any) of teaching bertsolaritza within the curricula of statutory schooling? In short, what price (if any) does bertsolaritza pay for its canonization?

Works Cited

Arin, N., & Satrustegi, I. (2020, March 5). Bertso eskolak, gozamenaren elkargune. *Berria*. Retrieved April 15, 2020, from https://www.berria.eus/paperekoa/1928/038/001/2020-03-05/bertso-eskolak-gozamenaren-elkargune.htm

Ariznabarreta, L. (2019). *Notes on Basque Culture: The Aftermath of Epics*. Montevideo: CLAEH.

Foley, J. M. (1998). The Impossibility of Canon. In J. M. Foley, *Teaching Oral Traditions* (pp. 13-33). New York: The Modern Language Association of America.

Garzia, J., Egana, A., & Sarasua, J. (2001). *The Art of Bertsolaritza. Improvised Basque Verse Singing*. Andoain: Bertsozale Elkartea.

Larrinaga, A., & Amurrio, M. (2016). The Ethno-linguistic Movement and Linguistic Self-determination in Euskara. In P. Ibarra Guell, & K. Ashild, *Basque Nationhood. Towards a Democratic Scenario* (pp. 83-119). Bern: Peter Lang.

Lujanbio, M. (2019). As the Tree Grows the Bark Cracks. In I. Arrieta Baro, & X. Irujo, *Female Improvisational Poets* (pp. 75-106). Reno: Center for Basque Studies Press.

Mindegia, M. (2019, February 7). Bertso eskolak bertsolaritzaren hauspo. *Noticias de Navarra.* Retrieved from https://www.bertsolari.eus/bertsolaritzaren-hemeroteka/bertso-eskolak-bertsolaritzaren-hauspo/

Mouillot, F. (2009). Resisting Poems: Expressions of Dissent and Hegemony in Modern Day Bertsolaritza. *Critical Studies in Improvisation/Etudes critiques en improvisation*, 5(1), 1-12.

Ruiz-Vieytez, E. J. (2016). Basque Sovereigntism and New Diversities in the Post-Violence Scenario. In P. Ibarra Guell, & A. Kolas, *Basque Nationhood. Towards a Democratic Scenario* (pp. 219-251). Bern: Peter Lang.

Scott, W. R. (2014). *Institutions and Organizations. Ideas, Interests, and Identities.* London: SAGE.

Appendix: Women Bertsolaris in a Time of Nuances: Bodies, Voices and the Art of Improvisation. An Interview with Maialen Lujanbio and Miren Artetxe

Reyes Lázaro, Smith College
Jacqueline Urla, University of Massachusetts Amherst

On February 6, 2018, Maialen Lujanbio and Miren Artetxe were invited to perform and talk about the growing presence of women in bertsolaritza at the Annie Boutelle Poetry Center of Smith College in Northampton, Massachusetts. They performed to a packed audience of students, professors and poetry lovers. It was a truly unforgettable event that allowed the audience to discover and appreciate the beauty of this form of cultural expression in Basque and to learn about the perspectives and experiences of women bertsolaris. After improvising in Basque, Maialen and Miren also improvised translations into English of what they had just sung. The audience was enthralled. In a particularly memorable moment, a student asked Maialen: "What reaction do you want to provoke in your audience when you sing?" Maialen gave us two answers that we feel capture the bertsolari spirit: [I want] to scratch (*arañar*) and to caress (*acariciar*).

The following interview was conducted during their visit at the Smith College recording studio by Reyes Lázaro (Spanish

Department, Smith College) and Jacqueline Urla (Anthropology, University of Massachusetts Amherst).[1]

Jackie: It is February 6, and we are at the recording studios of Smith College: Reyes Lázaro and myself, Jackie Urla. And we have with us, to our great pleasure, Maialen Lujambio and Miren Artetxe, two invited guests from the Basque Country, who will be performing and talking to us about bertsolaritza, a form of improvised poetry that's unique to the Basque Country. They are themselves poets and people who write about the influence of bertsolaritza and how it is changing today. We feel so lucky to have you here. Thank you for coming to visit us.

Maialen, Miren: Thank you!

Reyes: Until recently, it was not very common for women to participate in bertsolaritza. How did you come to be bertsolaris? What moments, people, or desires were especially decisive for you in taking this path?

Miren: Historical documents show that women were at one time prohibited from singing [bertsos]. We also have evidence beginning in the 19th century, of women winning championships. But once bertsolaritza becomes professionalized, and associated with a higher status; once it rises up from the public plaza to the stage, as it were, that is when women start to disappear. Now is when we are seeing a generation of women who have joined bertsolaritza. Maialen was the first.

Maialen: Well, [I'm] not the first, no, but in my case, what motivated me to start in bertsolaritza was not a family tradition. In my house no one was a bertsolari nor was there a special interest in bertsolaritza. But there was interest in my town, yes. The older bertsolaris – legendary ones like Txirrita – had a large presence. We have always sung his bertsos. They became almost

1 We are grateful to Ellen Watson, Director of the Annie Boutelle Poetry Center, and to Jeff Heath y Sandy Bicensky of Smith College for their technical assistance. A very special thank you to the Etxepare Institute and the William A. Douglass Chair in Basque Cultural Studies at University of Massachusetts Amherst that sponsored this visit. This interview has been edited and translated from the Spanish original by Lázaro and Urla.

traditional songs. So the presence [of bertsolaritza] was definitely there. I don't know exactly what motivated me. Probably my fascination/love for the language that I have had since I was a child. That interest in the language, in Euskara, in the language for playing, for writing… and in singing. I have always liked to sing very much.

Probably the most important element was the creation of the bertso-eskolak, afterschool workshops where boys and girls are taught how to improvise. I remember that in my ikastola there was a bertso-eskola. I knew people who were starting to sing in bertso-eskolas. Maybe that was the spark. I remember that I started on my own, composing bertsos – or something like them -- on my own. Seeing that I liked this language-work, our teacher proposed to us that we start in the bertso-eskola of the ikastola (grammar school). And that is how I started. You never know if it is just random. But I can say that [in my case[it definitely was not a result of family transmission or anything like that.

Miren: In my case, my grandfather was a big fan and through him, my father was as well. The memory that I have before entering bertso-eskola is of when we would go by car to the house of our grandparents. It was about half an hour away. We would go singing: my father would sing a verse, and me the next, "puntuka" style (rhyme by rhyme). I rhymed when I could, but it was like a game. I liked to play with words a lot. In our family the language was not just for communicating concepts; it was also for playing. When the bertso-eskola was created in our ikastola, for me it was obvious that it was made for me (laughs). So I started, but it was like a game, an afterschool activity. I didn't think of the bertso-eskola as a cultural world. It was nothing more than a game. Later you start to understand little by little what you are getting into.

Reyes: What is special about bertsolaritza in comparison to other forms of poetic improvisation (rap, repentismo, etc.)?

Jackie: Is there something unique about it? Have you had much exposure to other forms of improvisation?

Miren: I don't know much about slam or what we might call less traditional forms. Yes, we have been in contact with many other types of oral improvisation -- the decimas of Cuba, payadores of Argentina and Uruguay, the glosadores of Catalonia, regueiseros of Galicia. We have been in touch with other types of improvisational traditions of other countries and other languages, especially in Spanish, but also in other languages. They have different structures, coming from different social traditions. Each culture gives its own symbolic value to its oral improvisation. In our case, in 2003, there was a reflection about this that maybe for me is a bit self-righteous (I don't know if I should say this). It was concluded that the topical or thematic range in basque oral tradition is broader in comparison with other improvisational forms that are more tied to tradition, narrowly understood. For example, [in bertsolaritza], you can be asked to speak as if you were a bottle half empty (or half full) of anything. You can sing from the perspective of that subject. Also, [when it comes to] the degree of improvisation, there are not as many formulas as in other types of improvisation.

Maialen: The difference in the practice of the art is that in the Basque Country the thematics are more concrete, and the format is more dialectical in nature compared to traditions that are more lyrical or rhetorical. Ours is more dialectical and is based more on the argument. For that reason, I would say that ours is more rooted in the realities of particular places and moments. All improvisational traditions are based on this, but in our case it is very concrete, very dialectical and very argument oriented. It is also unquestionably tied to the situation of the language, and, in the end, to the situation of the country or place. I don't know if this connection is as tight in other improvisational traditions.

Miren: I see many more things in common with other oral improvisational traditions than things that set us apart or make us special. In general, the problematic that we share, especially with other improvisational traditions of minoritized languages, is that the questions, the debates, are more or less the same.

Reyes: Is the relationship with the audience also similar?

Miren: We do share a similar interest/concern in our relationship with the audience.

Jackie: How do you train to sing, to be a bertsolari? You have talked about bertso schools. Can you give us an idea of what is done in the bertso school and also what you do outside of it? How do you train to be a good bertsolari?

Maialen: Yes, I think this is an interesting question because on the one hand there is the basic technical preparation that anyone can acquire with training. That is what you would learn in the bertso-eskola that consists, for example, in the technique for improvising, which is to start the bertso with the final argument that people will hear at the end. It is assumed that what is said at the end is what has the most impact. The bertsolari, he or she, thinks first about the ending and that ending gives you the rhyme. You structure that idea in a particular meter and you start to construct the bertso backward – starting with the end and going to the beginning, from the bottom to the top. Then you begin the pure improvisation, moving along the tightrope, going toward the second rhyme and from there, little by little, towards what you had previously semi-prepared or imagined [for the end]. Your ending should be something fresh, unexpected. After that comes the next part of learning and developing., which is really interesting. Anyone can learn how to improvise, just as anyone can write a story. It is another thing to be a good writer.

How is it done? I don't know; it is a very abstract thing. This training is, in my case, to pay attention to what is around you, think about topics, problems that interest you, affect you, that are happening. It involves thinking, or developing a point of view on these problems, locating yourself in reality or in relation to these problematics. [It means to] take a position, think about what you want to say and to work on that subjectivity or point of view, opinions, nuances, what is being said and also maybe what you don't agree with. What seems like a slogan that you want to challenge? What is politically correct, what is not correct? ... what can I say and what can't I say, always having the audience in mind because, of course, the public does not let you say just anything. They have to understand you. Your goal is to communicate and so you have to deliver something they can digest. The audience varies. And a topic that might interest you might not sit well with a particular audience. You have to learn how to deliver the right amount, find the way to express yourself in the specific context in which you find yourself. A rural festival is not the same as a gaztetxe [youth cultural association], etc. You have to adapt to the context and, this is important, without losing your principles, saying what you want to say. It is a form of gymnastics.

Miren: And you have to do all of that while rhyming every 18 syllables. (laughter)

Maialen: She and all of us. It is an important struggle. It is not often that you end up feeling satisfied and happy. Improvisation, because it is improvisation, always has an element of imperfection. It is never perfect. If it were written, maybe it would be perfect. There is always the possibility of misunderstanding. There is always that feeling of "I didn't say it well," "I didn't say it sufficiently clearly or powerfully," or "I went too far." You are always negotiating with the audience and with yourself. And, apart from that, the most important thing is that you can't always say everything you would like to say because you are improvising, and the rhyming doesn't let you. Or maybe the idea is too complex for the shortness of the meter in which you have to work. It is a constant struggle and also a constant balance that you must achieve between the aesthetics, the rhyming meter, the [need to] communicate, the argument. This cannot be avoided. You have to say things that are intelligible, that can be assimilated. You have to look for elements that are as balanced as possible.

Jackie: In an interview you say that when you compose a bertso you do not try to have everything overly clear and concrete. Can you say more about this?

Maialen: I don't know when I said that, but probably it was provoked by a certain way of composing bertsos that has been very sharp, very sloganeering (I don't want to disparage anyone), airtight and absolute. We [bertsolaris] come out of that style of arguing grand ideas that motivate the audience. I'm exaggerating to make a point. I have tried not to be so pretentious and not to sing truths, arguments or reasons from the position of "the Truth" in that very absolutist way. I have tried, or try, because as I said, this is a constant struggle, also with myself, including in these topics, between what I think and what I can say. I am more interested in the nuances. I think that for bertsolaris our role is to work on the nuances more than the grand reasons or grand truths. I think that our role is to focus on the point of view and look at the big problems, at reality, from a poetic, personal and developed perspective that can feed into official discourses and truths that are already out there. I think our charge has to do more with the nuances of point of view. That was probably what I was thinking about.

Reyes: In that sense, do the subtleties of meaning become more apparent in the middle of the poem? In the journey to reach that endpoint that you first thought of and planned? Is this middle ground, when you don't know exactly how you will get to that end, the space of improvisation?

Maialen: Yes, the question of how the subtleties of meaning emerge—whether it comes at the end or during the most pure improvisation --I think it is both. It is also interesting because you have twenty or thirty seconds to decide where you are going to locate yourself vis a vis a topic that is often delicate. Then you have to transmit that through the microphone. The complexity is not something that you improvise. You have thirty seconds and you will undress yourself. Your subconscious or unconscious will emerge. Either you prepare in advance and have your ideas clear or somewhat clear or that will be very apparent. Sometimes you slip up and sometimes improvisation takes you to places you did not want to go. But you have to be prepared (....). If you don't work on this... you might sing something that later you do not like.

Miren: I don't know if the subtleties of meaning are due to the format of the poem or to the evolution of society. It is like the relationship between painting and photography. Bertsolaritza used to have the role of communicating information, stories, to be a bit like the troubadours that sang the popular version of certain narratives. Now we have new modes of communication: Twitter, Youtube. Bertsolaritza does not need to play this function and so we have the freedom of providing particular perspectives, counterpoints. I agree with Mailaen that this is the most interesting role [of bertsolaritza] today. I don't know if it is so much because of the format of improvisation or whether it is because these functions are already being carried out and we don't have the responsibility any longer.

Reyes: When you say "worked on" or prepared in advance, what do you mean – work outside of the performance? (Do you call it a "performance"?)

Maialen and Miren: Yes, performance.

Reyes: Outside of the performance?

Maialen: Yes, outside [the performance]. Because it is about your ideology, [your] thinking about the themes. You might get asked about an issue. You don't have to have it formally prepared, but you must have thought about it so that it doesn't catch you by surprise.

Miren: For example, in an article that talks about migrants, if you see condescension you will try not to reproduce it in your bertsos. If you have not identified this, you will repeat it.

Jackie: In that sense, the bertsolari seems to be a social observer, a commentator, someone who observes and takes positions. Is that right?

Maialen: Yes, yes, yes. And then also we aim to do it without being pretentious. We don't always speak about the political conflict or about economic inequality or migration. We also talk about specific problems in specific contexts. For example, that they want to build a road in this or that town. But the attitude is the same: it is to observe the context, the specific place, the specific town, listen to the people, what they say, and to see what there is there, and then express it in a poetic manner, effective, with humor.

Miren: It can even be a situation where two people are hooking up in a discotheque. There is an element of ideology in how you position yourself, how you speak... All of this you have to have worked out in your mind in order to say what you want to say, and not to say something that you will regret later.

Maialen: Yes, because the inertia of memory plays a role: what we already know, all the previous bertsos we have heard, television, films... our heads are full of that...

Reyes: of 'doxa'

Maialen: Yes, and if you don't reflect on this, if you don't notice or work on it, you will say it out of the inertia of memory. Maybe you are saying things you don't even realize, if you think twice. And that is very frustrating. "But I don't think like that?"

Reyes: I want to ask you a question about the body. A trapeze artist who walked between the twin towers in New York, Phillipe Petit, once came here for a visit. I remember that he spoke about the moment of grabbing the bar in his hands and forging ahead to walk into the void. I think that you do something similar. I would like you to tell us a little about how you experience your body as improvisers.

I also want to read something by Oteiza to get your reaction: "the technique of the bertsolari is to be in front of everyone and to disappear into their own reality. Out of [this internal reality] their words emerge (will continue emerging), as if letting themselves be carried along submerged in a river (the river of their interior vision)".[2] Do you see yourselves in that description? Can you talk to us about your body and your mind when you are in front of an audience [and] you take the bar and say, "there I go!"?

Miren: On the one hand, I do feel very identified with this. It is a little like that. But in the citation, the body is rendered invisible. It's as if the bertsolaris only had a voice and a mind. But the body is now a battleground in bertsolaritza. There is another angle to my opinion. Women have certain problems... when it comes to stepping into the void to do your own show of tightrope walking. I identify two moments. One in which I am empowered and feel like I'm going to do it well and others when I feel my body because I'm sweating, my voice is trembling ... and in that moment I am much more aware of the vulnerability of my body and I am tied to what I am saying. [With regard to the quote from Oteiza] I would say yes, it is like entering an interior world, but you can't do it without the body. I think the two are linked.

Maialen: Yes, yes. I agree but I think that in my case I have not been very aware of my body, I think, of the body. I do identify strongly with Oteiza's words. Nowadays we are analyzing the role of the body in front of the audience, on the stage, the woman's body on the stage, and [also] the voice. I haven't been that conscious of it I think. I have identified with and felt good in this almost immaterial, neutral body, as if [my] body did not exist. This has given me a lot to think about, because I have not had this battle – at least not consciously, with myself. I haven't been aware of being in my body. I have been aware of the voice but not the body. Now we are paying attention to this and I'm a little lost. Not "lost," but it is not something I've thought a lot about.

Miren: Well, I also have not always been so conscious of my body either. We've spoken about bertsolaritza as if the body did

2 Garzia, Joxerra, Jon Sarasua, and Andoni Egaña. 2001. *The Art of Bertsolaritza: Improvised Basque Singing*. Donostia: Bertsozale Elkartea, p. 25.

not exist. Now I think: how have I been able to be improvising without being aware of my body? Now that we are more aware that the body exists, I feel like I'm noticing it all the time. How could we have ignored it?

Maialen: We have done more reflection on the voice, inevitably. And yes, we have done a small amount of reflecting on it from the point of view of gender: what voices get recognized? What voices are respected? Seen as interesting voices? What themes are seen to be interesting? This has been theoretically analyzed a bit more. The more agile, refined voices [of women] have been valued less, because men have been able to sing from more sensitive voices. For women this has been a hándicap. There is a profound and interesting analysis to be had [about this].

Miren: In effect, women were not told, "You cannot sing because you are a woman." Women were told instead that their voice was not right. Of course, the voice was a metonym for the body.

Reyes: When it comes to singing, where does the musical element fit in? Do you have to sing well? Do you have to be able to sing? To have a good ear?

Maialen: I think that –from my perspective – which is what I always give (laughter) – is that you have to sing well. The thing is that to sing bertsos well is not the same as singing in a choir, to sing opera, pop, or canto. Singing bertsos well is another thing. In fact, the people that can sing opera well, tend to be too "singer-ly" [*cantada*]. People will criticize a performance if it is too "*cantada*." The verb we bertsolaris use is not exactly "to sing," but rather "bertsoa bota" which means to "throw" out a verse. We don't use the verb "to sing." This is significant in itself, no? There are very "authentic" voices, very aligned with the persona of the person singing, with the body, that may not be singing "well" in the lyrical or musical sense, but which are super effective, and have a lot of power. Yes, you have to sing well, but not in musical terms, but in bertsolaritza terms. It is not enough to only sing well. Everyone has to find their way of communicating, their way of making themselves heard, their tone of voice, their volume. You have to find it. And when you find it and it works, well, that, for me, is what it means to sing well.

Miren: And then, "to sing well" is always tied to a particular time and place. Fifty years ago what it would have meant to sing well, without microphones, etc., was different. People sang differently, even in bertsolaritza, which had a different social role. To sing well was different [in the past]. To sing well is always something tied to a particular social and historical moment. It also has a gendered dimension, of course. The act of making oneself heard, and the criteria that are used in judging whether a person makes themselves heard or not, that is gender specific.

Maialen: Yes, we also see in the world of music, including rock, pop…women have to sing well. Men can sing in many different ways, even singing badly they can have a lot of personality. But it seems like women have to sing well. And in our case, it is probably the same. But, on the other hand, I would say today we don't attend enough to the song, to the sung part of the bertso. We don't concern ourselves with the fact that what we are doing is singing, and in front of an audience. The sung part has tremendous importance and I think that we are not paying enough attention to that. We are putting all our attention on the message, which is good, in the content, but that content is sung. You have to find a way to convey with power, efficiently, and make yourself heard, and the medium is singing.

Reyes: Why does it have to be sung?

Maialen: Standard bertsolaritza is sung improvisation. That is essential. We should not neglect that. Many times we are focused on the message or the ideology that we should not forget, but the medium of the transmission is the song.

Miren: I think it is sung because the melody is shared by the singer and the listener. Having this in common makes communication more effective. In rap there is rhyme, there is structure but it can be so flexible that the thread that connects the listener and the performer is thin. Here, with the melody known by everyone, not just me and the bertso, but rather the whole acoustic space that receives the melody like a shared common space with the audience, this makes the thread that connects us broader, stronger.

Reyes: I would like to read another quote with various metaphors to describe a bertsolari. "The bertsolari plays a role somewhere between the social and the poetic, between leader and fool, between columnist and satiric newspaper cartoonist, while at the same time remaining an ordinary member of their own social world."[3] Which of these various roles do you personally identify with or do you have other metaphors? How do you imagine your social role as bertsolaris?

Maialen: I really like that quote. Yes, I do identify with this. The bertsolari is an interesting figure. They are part of society but an observer. They can have a very sophisticated vision but they also draw on humor, and diversion, pure and simple. Humor is a very big part of it that we shouldn't disregard. Bertsolartiza covers many dimensions, registers, levels. They are an artist that comes from that audience, is a part of the audience. I think this is very interesting from a sociocultural perspective.

Jackie: We are here at the Poetry Center of a women's college to do an exhibition of bertsolaritza, focusing on the role of women and their entry into this form of improvisation. I'd like to give you the opportunity to comment on how you see the greater presence of women to be affecting the image or themes of bertsolaritza (or whatever else you think is interesting about this).

Maialen: I think that when we young women started singing, at first it was very much anecdotal, an oddity, a curiosity. Little by little, over time, as women, through their work and voice, started for the first time playing the roles of women – before men used to play the women; they gave them a voice – for the first time, the role of a woman is played by a woman, [she] uses other discourses, another reality that causes men to have to step aside. The arguments change. Everything becomes more complicated, in other words, more interesting. The place of men

3 Garzia, Joxerra, Jon Sarasua, and Andoni Egaña. 2001. *The Art of Bertsolaritza: Improvised Basque Singing*. Donostia: Bertsozale Elkartea, p. 61.

has shifted a lot. Little by Little, with the years and a more self-aware or feminist discourse, women and the discourse of women have started to have a greater presence. And this has shifted the whole terrain. First, our colleagues have had to adapt, revise their positions. The themes have changed a lot. The realities of the discourse have also changed because women use their voice. There has emerged a fairly large number of women, young women of varied profiles, who bring different discourses, different characteristics, just in the last few years. This is a very interesting moment in bertsolaritza. I think we are experiencing a small revolution, a small earthquake, just as happened in the past. Now the next one is coming, with the entrance of women, more diverse and more self-aware. The discourse, forms, themes and dialogues are changing and alongside this the bertsolaris and the audience. Everything little by little, eh? But I think that is what is taking place.

Miren: I completely agree. With the first incorporation of women like Maialen in her time, the archetypical woman now becomes a body. The structure changes, is transformed a little. At that time it was like: "Okay, we let women join in bertsolaritza. Even though they are women, they can sing." That was the first stage. Later the bertso-eskolas started, when everything seemed to be in danger of disappearing. We needed everybody's help. Then women start to join in and there is a small revolution. Then structural problems start to emerge and a feminist analysis is done of the situation. Women start to come together, we realized that we were all asking ourselves the same questions. We realized that men didn't have the same kinds of limits on their humor as we did. We realized that the rules of the game were not the same. (...). Today we have a pretty sophisticated feminist analysis of bertsolaritza. And that coincides with the figure of Maialen par excellence. She has won two times in what is considered classic bertsolaritza, and that is changing the cannon. At the same time, there is a new generation that is doing their own analysis... they want to change things. There is a convergence. These two elements are coming together. It is an interesting time.

Reyes: Does this have any impact on the vision of this genre, bertsolaritza, as a battle between poets? Has the entrance of women influenced the understanding of bertsolaritza as a verbal duel, a confrontation?

Miren: Yes, yes. [The anthropologist] Jone Miren Hernández says that right now bertsolaritza is in a process of renegotiation. Two examples: when Maialen tries to convey her truths or convey her meanings, then confrontation loses power. Something else is happening on stage. The cannon is changing. Others are joining the discourse. And when you are singing about emotions you cannot tell someone, "you don't feel that." So confrontation in itself is not very relevant. So, on the one hand, that is changing. On the other hand, all-women performances are being created, and we have realized that we don't sing the same. Before, all-women performances were only done on March 8. In those situations we didn't have the burden of being the only woman on the stage. When you are the only one, it's not so easy to be the buffoon, to be ridiculous or vulgar. You cannot because you represent all women. But when we are seven women on stage, we can each choose who we want to be. So while we don't want to enter into the debate about whether there is specific women's bertsolaritza, we do say that the dynamics are changing. Right now, to describe bertsolaritza as a form of confrontation between two discourses (performers) doesn't really capture it. Between the experiences of this generation of women and the cannon that Maialen is changing…

Reyes: I would like to ask you to speak about each other – what impresses you about each other?

Maialen: How much time do I have? (laughter). Okay, I'll start. It is just that I have not sung very much with Miren. We have coincided very little because she has had a period of silence. But luckily, she is back and... Lucky us! As you have been able to see, her perspective and analytical capacity are impressive.

I think it is vital today. I think that a point of view like hers, analytical, critical, elaborated, is fundamental including for me. In this small earthquake, we are all moving, not just others. I myself have been very critical of the existing structure, but I have also felt very comfortable in it. Miren and other groups of women are collectively doing ideological work and causing all of us to shift. Including me. For me this is super interesting. It will be uncomfortable for me, but very interesting. It will cause me to question my forms and my inertias, what I have done well and not so well. Miren is indispensable in this momento of bertsolaritza. And what makes me the happiest is that she has returned to singing. It is not just the critical theoretical point of view but the critical theoretical view put into practice. Singing, with her body and her voice. Miren is a fundamental and super interesting part of this really interesting moment we find ourselves in.

Miren: As she always tells me: great idea, but tell it to me in 18 syllables (laughter). I will breathe a little. Me, what could I say about Maialen? So many things. To start with, only she could do what she had done. To be there [in bertsolaritza], since she was very young, enduring, enjoying… I don't think it was [necessarily] a sacrifice [for her], but it would have been a very big sacrifice for many people. Endure, enjoy,… she has done this with so much agility, changing things from the beginning. On the other hand, we have been talking about a feminist generation, but that generation would not have been possible without the figure of Maialen. Maialen is changing the cannon of bertsolaritza and she is taking it to a much more interesting place than where it was previously. It was already interesting and now it is much more so. She has incorporated the concept of subjectivity. She is taking bertsolaritza to a very productive terrain that has been unexplored until now. As a result, Maialen has made the space of bertsolaritza much more livable for many of us. That is why I and many others can come back and sing, because bertsolaritza is now a space where you can feel much more comfortable. And there is her way of locating herself vis a vis the world that interests me. I am interested in what Maialen thinks. I could keep talking for hours.

Jackie: Could you elaborate a bit more about this issue of subjectivity? How is this different from the bertsolaritza of the past? What has changed?

Miren to Maialen: You have to help me.

Maialen: Well, I have not theorized about this. I do what I do intuitively and then the analysis is usually done later by others.

Miren: To explain the evolution, I'm going to simplify. Let's say that before they would tell [the bertsolari] "you are a doctor." What the bertsolari aimed to do was to portray the stereotype of the doctor that the public might have -- of the doctor with his bag, his white coat, education, social class... [as the bertsolari] you would be successful the more you conveyed that stereotypical image. By contrast, Maialen began to sing about a female doctor, 25 years old, [she conveyed] her idea of a doctor, someone still learning to practice, and that changed the idea. She elaborated and created characters and subjectivities very clearly portrayed that had not existed before. It is said that Maialen "sings from herself" as if the others did not. Now you are obliged to position yourself. That began to be valued because of Maialen. Of course, it is not really so simple. Before, there were other subjectivities, but not in such a conscious way.

Jackie: Could you talk to us about how you see bertsolaritza fitting into the Basque language revival movement?

Maialen: (...) I think that bertsolaritza has become a referent in the language movement because it has had a good strategy and vision that has proven to be successful. Today is the day that it is the most popular cultural practice in the Basque Country. It has based its success on a vision that does not fear taking risks, making changes, experimentation and innovation, because we have nothing to lose; we can only improve. This has been a great stance, this decision to open ourselves and experiment without losing our compass, without losing our self-esteem, being self-aware but taking risks and innovating. Bertsolaritza has become a modern activity, contemporary, without any inhibition about collaborating in any contemporary activity. It attracts young people. It can adapt to any space, any context. (…) In general terms, I would say that the vision and practice of bertsolaritza have been spot-on, and it is [a strategy] that we would want as Basque speakers to be reproduced in other domains, whether in the language domain or others.

Reyes: What is the relationship today between bertsolaritza and rock music, with young people, with the urban and the rural worlds? Sorry, I know these are big questions.

Maialen: The good thing is that there is not a dichotomy. We have won spaces without losing older ones. We have not lost the rural. We still sing one day in a super urban space, super underground, and the next day… it is completely normal. Friday, you go to one place, and Saturday, to another. You can be accepted, listened to, and part of both. What is interesting is that we have won spaces without losing what we had before. The same is true with audiences. We have gained young people, urban, alternative, who were not of our same context, without losing the traditional audience. And that is good. Super variable profiles. In the audience there might be children, parents, grandparents – such different people enjoying the same activity is something that does not happen in practically any other cultural activity.

With regard to [your question about] rock or rap, bertsolaritza today can be in conversation with any contemporary cultural practice, from plastic arts to music, literature, theatre, film. We have collaborated on all kinds of activities. Nowadays it is very common, although still relatively new, but nowadays it is not rare to have a rock group adopt bertsos or collaborate with us.

Jackie: To conclude, could you talk about how you see the current moment and what challenges does it present you with as artists?

Maialen: From an artistic point of view I think this is a very interesting time. Before we were in a moment of grand truths and grand resistance or counter truths [relating to] the armed conflict and the political conflict. We had the "great problem" that still has not been fully resolved. As Miren said, bertsolaritza always has played a very interesting role as counterinformation against official discourse; [it has been] 'the voice' in quotation marks, of the people. This terrain of alternative communication has been very interesting. Now, things have become more complicated, diffuse, and require more nuances and concrete ideas. Among ourselves it is often said that it is difficult to generate the emotions of the audience as we used to with a grand, epic, romantic idea that has everyone jumping to their feet. There was this historical moment of resistance and accumulated pain, a tension that we still have today. Artistically, this engendered a style of grand truths and grand countertruths, of large monolithic and fixed ideas. This is not that interesting artistically. It was difficult to introduce nuances, because if you did that, then you had to do it for everything. Sometimes when faced with the [political] conflict and the pain you opt for great counter-truths. You say to yourself, "I am not 100% in agreement with that idea but I have to say it because it is an idea that should also be heard, because it is an idea that challenges the official discourse, for example. I'm speaking in general.

But this [stance] lacked nuance. That is why people say that we are in a more complex moment. Everything is "yes, but." Today it is said that the audience is also more difficult. It is more difficult to touch a nerve, to reach their hearts with the idea of Euskal Herria or Euskara. But today's situation is much more interesting. It is the era of nuances, criticism and self-criticism. Of criticism of criticism. You can contribute other ideas and other colors. Also the range of topics has expanded greatly. Today the political, ideological, social include many more themes. (…) Before there was only one topic: "politics." Now politics is in everything. Topics have emerged that were unimaginable. Now ideology is in everything, it is like real life. Now is the time of nuances and not of standing ovations but rather big discomforts. And this is very interesting.

Miren: In terms of historical evolution, we could say that at first bertsolaritza was sung before a relatively homogenous audience with a much more shared way of life and cosmovision than now. It has been diversifying but we still preserve some basic ideological orientations. And today (as you say) the era in which those grand ideas could move an audience has passed. Everything is much more complex; at the same time, bertsolaritza will decide, and has to decide, to what degree it will also seek to make visible the Conflict, because it has not disappeared. These issues have been rendered invisible by politics with a capital "P." It is an interesting moment socially.

Reyes: Euskal Herria is fortunate to have you as artists, bertsolaris, theorists. From what you have said, you embody the fundamental principle of improvisation, which rather than "yes, but" is "yes, and..."

Maialen: What a luxury of an interview. We would be happy to have more kinds of interviews like this.

www.ingramcontent.com/pod-product-compliance
Lightning Source LLC
LaVergne TN
LVHW010058110826
845155LV00028B/388

* 9 7 8 1 9 4 9 8 0 5 6 4 2 *